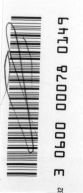

WRITERS AND POLITICS
IN MODERN SPAIN

Writers and Politics in Modern Spain

John Butt

Holmes & Meier Publishers, Inc.
New York.

Writers and Politics in Modern Spain is one of a series of books under the general editorship of Professor John Flower. The other books in the series are as follows:

Writers and Politics in Modern Britain (J. A. Morris)
Writers and Politics in Modern France (J. E. Flower)
Writers and Politics in Modern Germany (C. E. Williams)
Writers and Politics in Modern Italy (J. A. Gatt-Rutter)
Writers and Politics in Modern Scandinavia (Janet Mawby)

First published in the United States of America 1978 by
Holmes and Meier Publishers, Inc.
30 Irving Place, New York, N.Y. 10003

Library of Congress Cataloging in Publication Data

Butt, John.
    Writers and politics in modern Spain.

    Bibliography: p.
    1. Spanish literature – 20th century – History and
criticism. 2. Politics and literature – Spain.
3. Politics in literature. I. Title.
PQ6073.P6B8   860'.9'0064   78–18704
ISBN 0–8419–0415–4

Printed in Great Britain by
Cox & Wyman Ltd,
London, Fakenham and Reading

Foreword

The term 'political literature' like 'committed literature' with which it is frequently associated has become an accepted part of the language of literary history. Yet however convenient, it is, on examination, surprisingly imprecise and misleading. The whole area of the interaction between politics and literature is a vast and complex one which has yet, especially on a European scale, to be fully and comprehensively charted. Certainly invaluable contributions do already exist: Jean-Paul Sartre's *Qu'est-ce que la littérature?* (1947), George Woodcock's *The Writer and Politics* (1948), Jürgen Rühle's *Literatur und Revolution* (1960), Irving Howe's *Politics and the Novel* (1961), John Mander's *The Writer and Commitment* (1961) for example. There are too, as the bibliographical information contained in the individual essays in this series will reveal, a number of equally important books which deal with the issue in purely national terms. With few exceptions, however, these, like many of the more general studies, suffer from the same defects resulting in the main from a failure to distinguish adequately between 'political literature' and what might be termed 'social literature', and from an incomplete assessment of changes both in political climates and in the writer's relationship to society as a whole. Yet, even when the area of investigation and terminology has been more carefully ascertained, we often find that these books are principally concerned either with an examination of the political ideas *per se* contained in various works of literature, or with an assessment of the ways in which parties and movements have controlled and used to best advantage writers and intellectuals who claim political allegiance. More recently Roland Barthes in *Le Degré Zéro de l'écriture* (1967), George Steiner in *Language and Silence* (1967) and David Caute in *Illusion* (1971) have suggested a wider perspective, outlining some of the problems of style and form which an imaginative writer has to face when he offers his pen to a political (or social) cause. On the whole, however, it is fair to say that the majority of critics have concentrated more on *what* ideas are expressed than on *how* they have been. In addition therefore to attempting to define the concept of political literature more precisely and to exploring such issues as the suitability of imaginative literature as a vehicle for political ideas or the effect such literature can have on the public for example, one of the principal concerns of these essays is to attempt to examine ways in which an author's political sympathy or affiliation can be seen to affect or even dictate the way in which he writes. In some countries—in Russia, France or Spain, for example—direct influence of this kind is more apparent than in others. Elsewhere, notably in Britain, where political directives concerning art and literature have not been the rule, the problem is in some ways more difficult to assess. Indeed national variation of this kind is one of the principal contributory factors to the complex nature of the whole question. Thus while the subject is best illustrated and examined in the literature of France and Germany during the interwar years, it is after the Second World War that it fully emerges in the works of Italian and Scandinavian writers. Furthermore literary experiment seen and approved in some countries as an expression of a progressive, even revolutionary, political position is considered in others to be characteristic of subversion and decadence.

Given such problems as these and given too the amount of space available, these small volumes can do little more than hope to encourage a new approach to political literature. While free to explore the subject in the way they believe to be most useful within the context of the literary history of their particular countries, contributors have been encouraged to balance general comment with examination of specific examples. Inevitably therefore the essays appear arbitrarily selective. But like the literature which they choose to examine it is hoped that they will be judged not only for what they contain but also for the ways in which they deal with it.

John Flower

General Bibliography

The following are a selection of those books which discuss some of the general problems associated with this subject. Suggestions for further reading are contained in the notes to individual essays.

BARTHES, Roland, *Le Degré Zéro de l'écriture*, Editions du Seuil, Paris, 1953 (Translated: *Writing Degree Zero*, Cape, London, 1967).

CAUTE, David, *Illusion: An Essay on Politics, Theatre and the Novel*, Deutsch, London, 1971.

CROSSMAN, Richard, *The God that Failed: Six Studies in Communism*, Hamish Hamilton, London, 1950.

HOWE, Irving, *Politics and the Novel*, Horizon Press, New York, 1955.

MANDER, John, *The Writer and Commitment*, Secker & Warburg, London, 1961.

MUIR, Edwin, *Essays on Literature and Society*, Hogarth Press, London, 1965.

PANICHAS, George A. (ed.), *The Politics of Twentieth-Century Novelists*, Crowell, New York, 1974.

RÜHLE, Jürgen, *Literatur und Revolution*, Kiepenheuer & Witsch, 1960 (Translated: *Literature and Revolution*, Pall Mall, London, 1969).

SARTRE, Jean-Paul, *Qu'est-ce que la littérature?* Gallimard, Paris, 1948 (Translated: *What is Literature?* Methuen, London, 1951).

STEINER, George, *Language and Silence: Essays and Notes, 1958–66*, Faber, London, 1967.

TROTSKY, Leon, *Literature and Revolution*, University of Michigan Press, Ann Arbor, 1960.

WINEGARTEN, Renee, *Writers and Revolution: the fatal lure of action*, Franklin Watts, New York, 1974.

WOODCOCK, George, *The Writer and Politics*, The Porcupine Press, London, 1948.

Contents

Preface

In this short study I have attempted a general survey of the impact of the ideal of political commitment on the forms—particularly the language—of Spanish literature in the twentieth century. This has involved an excursion into a rather suspect field—literary history. But it seemed to me that a general approach was justified in the case of Spanish literature, because detailed consideration of individual writers' political beliefs would have involved cataloguing the attitudes of numerous authors unknown and inaccessible to the general reader whom I had in mind when writing.

Of all the literatures studied in this series, Spanish and Soviet literature in particular have been radically reshaped in their overall development in this century by ideas about political commitment. In the USSR, Socialist realism was eventually imposed as the official form of the literature of Communism. Only in Spain, therefore, were critical theories derived from political theories (most, but not all, Marxist or Marxian) spontaneously adopted by perhaps a majority of creative writers during a significant period of the country's literature (about 1950 to 1965). This makes the Spanish example unique. Soviet modernism was destroyed from above by Zhdanovite prescription; Spanish modernism was subverted from below, as a result of the widespread rejection by writers of any type of literature which savoured of 'elitism' or 'escapism'. During the period 1950 to 1965 a large proportion of the new output in Spanish poetry, plays and novels seemed to be moving in the direction of Soviet-style Socialist realism. This was done discreetly, of course: censorship ensured that such literature cloaked itself in innuendo and allusion, and it was called 'social' or 'civic' literature by its practitioners, who identified their anti-Franco commitment by such euphemisms as 'concern with contemporary problems' or 'rejection of dehumanized literature' and so on. But the stratagem was to a surprising extent successful, and for some ten years Spanish literature was engulfed by a wave of curiously flat and underwritten prose narrative and 'realist' poetry and drama designed to mobilize readers against the Franco regime.

3

It was inevitable and right that literature should be put to political use under the Franco regime. By the 1950s the nightmare interlude of triumphal *Te Deums*, concentration camps and firing squads had largely abated, but the country was still controlled by a philistine and ruthless alliance of soldiers, businessmen, Catholic and Fascist fanatics and a host of opportunists of every right-wing shade. In such circumstances, fine literature, which to some extent escaped the censors' more extreme intolerance, was bound to be exploited by the opposition as the only outlet for even a limited and veiled protest. But, as I hope to show, there were critical factors which determined the form that this politicized literature took; factors connected with an important and neglected literary tradition which pre-dated the Franco regime and had its roots in the 1930s and even earlier, in the eighteenth and nineteenth centuries. The Franco regime strengthened liberal and left-wing support for this tradition, but it was created by critics and authors, not by the Nationalist victory of 1939.

It consisted of a sustained and quite complex critical campaign against modernism (a term I use in a way unusual in Hispanic studies and explain in the first chapter). This predominantly left-wing campaign was extremely unfortunate for Spanish literature and goes a long way to explaining why the growing point of Hispanic literature shifted from Spain to Latin America in the post-War period.

After more than two centuries of decline, Spanish literature had been liberated from the ideals of direct moral and political responsibility by the modernist movement which penetrated Spain at the beginning of the present century and unleashed a wave of pent-up creative activity which suddenly raised Spanish literature from obscurity to international status. This 'second Golden Age' of Spanish literature, from 1900 to 1936, had a uniquely modernist identity: it was based almost exclusively on a rejection of the realist tradition and was characterized by bold experiments and innovations in every genre. Although Spanish modernism had its negative features, it was immensely creative in its brief life. But despite this, hardly any new writers after 1939 profited from or absorbed any of the lessons of Spanish modernism. The concept of social realism as the appropriate and perhaps exclusive form for liberal or left-wing literature succeeded in discrediting modernism as anti-humanist or bourgeois. An army of critics—right-wing as well as left—implanted in Spain the idea that modernism necessarily embodies a specific *ideology*

4

which, whatever it is, is incompatible with progressive or nationalist politics.

To put this development into perspective, I give a brief account of the history and effects of the ideal of political and social responsibility on Spanish literature in the period 1830 to 1936. This account is extremely compressed, but seemed necessary because Spanish literature is probably less well known to English readers than other European literatures. Even then I have omitted reference here and later to Spanish theatre, although the general argument is applicable to this genre as well. Suggestive experiments by modernist playwrights such as Lorca and Valle-Inclán in this, the weakest genre of modern Spanish literature, gave way after the Civil War to prosaic moralizing devoid of theatrical tension and impact—as Hispanists will surely agree who compare the works of, say, Buero Vallejo and Alfonso Sastre with pre-Civil War playwrights.

This general survey is followed by a description of the anti-modernist campaign, and of the way modernism was politicized by the patronage of Europe's most patrician elitist, José Ortega y Gasset. I hope this account will interest readers concerned with the general development of twentieth-century European literature and will not be too obvious for expert Hispanists. It often happens that when it rains in Europe it pours in Spain, and arguments which bear on the life of the whole continent are pushed to clarifying extremes across the Pyrenees. This seems to me to be true of the Spanish controversy about the political implications of modernism and realism.

A final remark may be unnecessary: it is easy for an English-speaking Hispanist to criticize Spanish political literature from a safe distance and in the name of 'art'. Looked at from the point of view of a writer daily exposed to arbitrary arrest, torture, corruption and other abuses, a sonnet to a rose or a book like *Finnegan's Wake* can in the heat of the moment look like an irrelevance or even a gratuitous insult. Such violent anti-aestheticism may be counter-productive, but it is not difficult to sympathize with the motives behind it.

Acknowledgments

I am grateful to the Central Research Fund of the University of London for a grant towards expenses incurred in the pursuit of some of the material discussed herein. I am particularly obliged to a number of colleagues and friends, particularly to Carmen Benjamin and Geraldine Scanlon, for several excellent remarks from which I have profited. None, however, can be held responsible for the views expressed in this essay. I have also availed myself of the labours of J. Lechner, whose *El compromiso en la poesía española del siglo XX* in two parts (Leiden 1968 and 1975) is an indispensable guide to the history of politicized Spanish poetry.

All translations of quotations are my own, and have no literary pretensions. Quotations are usually taken from easily available editions, but dates of first publication are given in the text or notes.

Chapter One

Writers and Social Responsibility in Modern Spain

Politics and literature can be, and generally are, mixed, but when writers become convinced of the contrary, they usually try to reject one or the other—even when they continue to write. The overall development of modern Spanish literature has been strongly influenced by controversy about the writer's social and political responsibilities, and this is not surprising in view of the extreme and violent nature of Spanish politics. On the whole, this controversy has never led to a formula which would allow writers to live with an easy social conscience about work which is complex and formally elaborate. In the very act of producing work which puts demands on its readers, the Spanish writer often finds himself criticized for his detachment from the urgent political problems of his day. With the massive polarization of political life in Spain which preceded and followed the Civil War, this dilemma became increasingly acute.

The richest period of modern Spanish literature, from 1900 to the Civil War, is on the whole characterized by an urge to escape from local social and historical preoccupations: the literary elite of that period concerned themselves only marginally with party politics—at least until 1930. Despite, or because of, the disillusions of the Second Republic and the Civil War itself, the next thirty years reflect a growing obsession with politics on the part of numbers of Spanish writers. This obsession coincides with what is commonly felt to be a decline in the quality of the literature, although in the last ten years a reaction has set in against the idea of committed literature, producing a different kind of writing which has much more in common with the work of the pre-Civil War years. What follows is an attempt to trace the history of the idea of commitment in Spain, and to touch on some of its artistic implications. It is impossible in so short a space to do more than sketch an argument about politics and literature; but I hope that an examination of a few well-known writers and critics will show

7

how excessive (though understandable) concern with the political effect of literature halted the growth of what was promising, by the early 1930s, to be a major European literature and caused writers to throw out the very critical premises on which that promise was based.

Although the establishment of the Franco regime was a political and moral disaster, it is not entirely clear why it should have been a literary disaster. This is not to say that literature is an area of activity unaffected by other events; but it seems to me that the usual explanations for the poverty of post-Civil War Spanish literature compared with the work of the period 1900–1936—censorship and the death or exile of most of the great pre-War writers—are only partly satisfactory. The disappearance of great writers does not prevent the emergence of new ones, nor does it remove the example of their work. Intellectual and political freedom alone do not seem to be the *sine qua non* of a rich literature, as Tsarist Russia, Primo de Rivera's Spain and most of the pre-twentieth-century world seem to indicate. If censorship is assumed to be the sole reason for the lifelessness of Spanish literature between 1940 and the 1960s, why was no brilliant *samizdat* literature produced or fine work printed abroad?[1] Literature comparable with that of the pre-War period began to appear in the 1960s with the novels of Luis Martín Santos, Juan Goytisolo (in his later novels) and others, but this resurgence in creative writing was not really accompanied by any dramatic change in political conditions. It was due, rather, to a resumption of the modernist tradition: literary theory altered in the 1960s, not General Franco or his censors, and the 'experimental' works of Juan Benet, José María Guelbenzu, Martín Santos, Juan and Luis Goytisolo and others were generated by a dissatisfaction with anti-modernism, not by the 'free' atmosphere of some post-Fascist liberalization, if such indeed there was before Franco's death. Liberalization might in fact have been expected to produce *more* political literature if censorship had really been damming up political frustration. In fact the late Franco era produced a wave of largely apolitical writing, a curious paradox explicable in part by the failure of committed literature in the 1950s and early 1960s.

An examination of the relationship between politics, literary criticism and literature in Spain reveals other reasons for the greyness of much Spanish writing between 1940 and the early 1960s. In a situation in which all humane energies are devoted to attacking a particular regime, demands are put on literature which narrow its range and discourage experimental writing. In the case of Spain, these demands unfortunately worked against the emancipation of language and imagination brought by modernism[2] at the end of the nineteenth century, an emancipation which was the source of most of what was best and most characteristic in Spanish literature between 1900 and 1936. When the language and techniques of modernism were found by later writers to be somehow inconsistent with moral or political seriousness, a return was made to the less fruitful examples of nineteenth-century Spanish literature or to the few non-modernist works of the present century, especially the novels of Pío Baroja. The examples of Jiménez, Lorca, Valle-Inclán and others were forgotten, and a most productive literary tradition fell into decline.

This argument must not be taken as implying that realism is intrinsically inferior to modernism: Balzac, Dickens and Tolstoy were not exactly set-backs in the history of literature. But the realist novelists of other countries profited, in the nineteenth century, from cultural and social advantages denied to the Spanish writers.

The Realist Bias of Spanish Romanticism

Nineteenth-century Spanish literature compares very poorly with that of the twentieth century. A single major novelist (Galdós), and one other major realist novel (*La Regenta* by Leopoldo Alas), two gifted but extremely minor poets (Bécquer and Rosalía Castro)—the balance sheet of one hundred years of Spanish literature is not impressive. But unless there is a neglected case for a total revaluation of Pereda, Emilia Pardo Bazán, Valera, Espronceda and Larra as major European writers, the charge must stand. Not even the most generous Hispanophile could maintain that Spain produced anything like, to take a rather arbitrary series of examples, Goethe, Wordsworth, Coleridge, Schiller, Baudelaire, Nerval, Mallarmé, Austen, George Eliot or Ibsen.

The reasons for this weakness are numerous and include the survival of simple-minded Catholic ideas at all levels and the proverbial absence of a strong middle class. But there are other reasons which are relevant to the present argument, linked with the conceptions prevailing in nineteenth-century Spain about the relationship between literature and society. Without going further into the question of the

9

interdependence of literary and social change, it seems to me that a major obstacle to the growth of nineteenth-century Spanish literature was the failure of Spanish romanticism, a failure symbolized by the relative strength of the Spanish realist novel of the century compared with lyric poetry. Nothing is so striking about nineteenth-century Spanish literature as its lack of *inwardness*. It is a literature which, with a few exceptions, is shorn of subjectivity—at least when compared with that of France or England. This externality explains not only the poverty of nineteenth-century lyric poetry in Spain, but also the rather crude psychology of even the best of the realists—a crudity which contrasts with the complexity of their social and political analyses.

Spanish romanticism in the 1830s was a limited affair, a late arrival in a backward society unprepared to absorb the full significance of the romantic movement. It was also a heavily politicized society. In the 1830s a violent conflict was raging between liberals and reactionaries, and in this phase of Spanish history it was inevitable that writers should apply themselves to the urgent question of the possibility of personal freedom in a repressive society. In some cases, notably Larra, and Espronceda in *El diablo mundo*, this enquiry produced intelligent and perceptive insights into the limits of liberalism. But the themes of Spanish romanticism were mostly held at this public level. There was no accompanying philosophical or critical revolution; no basic re-assessment of the role of the imagination in literature; no true insight into the creative potential of the semi- or unconscious mind; no significant rebirth of interest in neo-Platonic or gnostic ideas; no real debate about the limits of rationalism; no renewed interest in non-Christian or exotic cultures; no 'return to nature' or nature poetry; no systematic defence of Rousseaunian ideas about human innocence. The manifestoes of Spanish romanticism, such as they are, propose limited programmes for the achievement of what was only an aspect of romanticism elsewhere: a 'national' literature to supersede years of imitation of foreign models, and based on a revaluation of aspects of sixteenth- and seventeenth-century literature and that of the Middle Ages. Alcalá Galiano for example, in his preface to Rivas's *El moro expósito*,[3] limits his defence of romanticism almost exclusively to an apology for 'national' literature: he has no conception of organic form and seems to think that inspiration, spontaneity and literary nationalism are the same thing. In Mariano José de Larra we find a fine intelligence acutely aware of the complex transition his society was undergoing in the 1830s. Yet, even if, as D. L. Shaw has argued,[4] Larra was one of the romantics who experienced the 'metaphysical crisis', he had a basically 'social' idea of the significance of romanticism. His remarks about literature indicate that he was a kind of committed realist *avant la lettre*: he rejected gratuitous formalism and advocated a literature which should be 'born of experience and history', accessible to the 'ignorant multitudes' and both 'proselytizing' and 'propagandistic'.[5]

In Larra we see how the Spanish eighteenth-century notion that literature should stay close to public life and themes survived Romanticism and remained a basic premise of Spanish literary criticism even at a time when exoticism and fantasy were fashionable. The ideal of social responsibility went barely challenged until the end of the nineteenth century. The Spanish realist novel and the controversies it generated, were much more bound up with politics than in other countries. The extremely dull arguments between literary 'idealists' and realists which fill the latter half of the nineteenth century revolve not around the relationship between literature and imagination (as they might fruitfully have done), but around questions of propriety and decorum or the religious implications of realist and naturalist theories. Neither side really challenged a crude mimetic theory of art. Social and moral didacticism was taken for granted by both conservative 'idealists' and liberal realists such as Pardo Bazán, Galdós and Alas. This was not, in the latter case, didacticism in a crude sense—the common theme of the realists' case was that those incurable dreamers, the Spanish people, were out of touch with real life, and that detailed, objective studies of 'reality' were a precondition for national regeneration. But in this polarized debate a third case—that of art for art's sake—was scarcely represented, and some kind of Spanish Parnassianism or *l'art pour l'art* movement was indispensable if Spanish critics and writers were to learn the lessons of post-romantic literature in France and elsewhere.

An advance to this third position might have been made by Juan Valera. He constantly went beyond conventional denunciations of the sordidness of realism and naturalism to a rejection of the idea of realism itself. At many points we find him explicitly defending aestheticism. He claimed that the proper function of art is the expression of beauty, and his theoretical essays draw on Platonism and German idealism to defend a metaphysical aesthetic theory. For a number of reasons, however, Valera never really progressed to the kind of aestheticism which would have made Spanish writers sensitive to the works of Poe, Baudelaire, Gautier and the Symbolists. Valera welcomed, with reservations, the publication of Rubén Darío's *Azul* (1888)—the first true modernist work in Spanish literature—but did so without realizing, as Darío justly remarked, 'the ultimate implications of my attempt' (*'la trascendencia de mi tentativa'*).[6] Valera's genuine or diplomatic patriotism closed his mind to foreign 'novelties', and his criticism often relapses into pleas for decorum in literature. His aesthetic theory is also too much centred on Roman and Greek models to allow a real breakthrough to a post-realist aesthetic. It is true that in his lectures to the Madrid Ateneo on the philosophy of art he drew attention to the way literature communicates things of which the author himself may not be aware. (His apologies for this apparently outrageous proposition indicate the literary elite's ignorance of the non-discursive potential of literary language.[7]) But he never really grasped the central idea of post-romantic French theories about evocation and suggestion, and his critique of realism is ultimately based on distaste for crude imitations of 'real life'.

It should be noted that at this time 'aestheticism' was not yet considered reactionary as it was to be later. Alarcón, an ultra-conservative, thought that the doctrine of art for art's sake was linked with the decline of morals and the rise of socialism and other beliefs 'conspiring to undermine the foundations of society'. Nocedal, a Catholic, denounced it as 'detestable' since the function of literature is communication of truth 'as defined by the Church'.[8]

Crude anti-aestheticism infected poetic theory. A measure of the failure of aestheticism to penetrate late nineteenth-century Spain is given by the popularity of the two poets Ramón de Campoamor and Núñez de Arce. Both published significant definitions of poetry in the mid-1880s, and their texts represent an argument which re-appeared in a different form in the 1930s. Campoamor, in his *Poética* (1883), proclaimed that he found the idea of *l'art pour l'art* 'antipathetic': 'my constant intention has been to arrive at "art for the sake of ideas" (*el arte por la idea*) and to express the latter in ordinary language (*lenguaje común*) . . .' (p. 35). Truly lyrical poetry should reflect the author's personal sentiments 'related to the particular problems of his day' (p. 77).

Núñez de Arce took this position much further, and his ideas approach a defence of political commitment. In place of the 'solitary lyrical muse', he recommends a more 'virile' poetry: in a 'century of revolution when all is shaking ... poetry, if it is to be great and appreciated, must think, and reflect the ideas and passions and suffering and joy of the society wherein it lives; not sing like a bird in the wood, indifferent to all around it and always the same'.[9]

In his *Discurso sobre la poesía* (1887) he argued that Spanish poetry, after 'unrealistic' excursions into the pastoral and 'extraordinary perversions of taste' in the Baroque, had at last returned to the realism which characterized it in the Middle Ages. In a turbulent age of political upheaval it has at last abandoned fantasy and 'taken sides among the belligerents' (*tomó partido entre los beligerantes*).[10] In other words it is 'committed'. The quality of his poems, on 'Doubt', 'Darwin' and 'Dialogue between a Bourgeois and Demagogue' can be imagined.

Núñez de Arce's argument is reminiscent of Larra's in the 1830s, and this continuity is significant. It reflects an anti-aesthetic, anti-Baroque prejudice which predates the nineteenth century and has its roots in the criticism of the Spanish eighteenth century. It would of course be absurd to blame critics alone for the feebleness of much eighteenth- and nineteenth-century Spanish writing. Yet when all the other social, intellectual and economic reasons for the weakness are taken into account, there is still room for the observation that more than one hundred and fifty years of literary decline in Spain coincide with an overall tendency amongst critics to repudiate aestheticism or literature written in 'elitist' forms of language. Spanish literature in the seventeenth century had been characterized by the triumph of a brilliant and barely intelligible Baroque diction, and it was perhaps inevitable that such literature, which apparently sacrificed intelligibility for verbal effect, should be discredited when critics became preoccupied (after about 1740) with public affairs. The anti-Baroque reaction was powerful and long-lasting. In the nineteenth century, romantics demanded a literature which would reflect the life of the 'people' (*pueblo*) or nation. *Costumbrismo* and realism afterwards continued this campaign to close the gap between literature and ordinary life, so that by the end of the century the case for aestheticism was almost unheard. The anti-Baroque reaction never really became a plea for political commitment, since eighteenth- and nineteenth-century *political* theories were not consciously totalitarian and the idea that literature should defend only these theories could not arise. But the view that writers should be responsible for propagating sound religion, decorum, good taste and patriotism, or enlightened educational

13

theories, tolerance and social concern, dominated the nineteenth century. Such arguments were sufficient to bind writers to the condition that their work should be popular, educative and intelligible, and in an illiterate and backward society, popularity and intelligibility could only mean conformity to the tastes and expectations of a narrowly based readership largely bourgeois or aristocratic in origin. The 'social' bias of such views thus meant the triumph of a specific literary language, symbolized by the 'Academy' Spanish of the age, with its latinate constructions and after-dinner rhetoric that survive in Establishment journalism even in the present day.

'Modernismo', 'Generation of '98' Avant-garde and Modernism in Twentieth-Century Spain

A few courageous breaks with the dominant mode were made somewhat before its consecration in the 1870s and 1880s. The most significant of these was by Gustavo Adolfo Bécquer, whose poems declare their own subject matter to be experience which transcends the outer world. Bécquer introduced into Spain in the late 1860s aspects of romantic interest in occultism, dream, memory and correspondences, which were absent in Spanish romanticism in the 1830s. Furthermore, he realized that new experience requires a new language and proposed in his first *Rima* the creation of one inspired by colour and music. But the overall effect of his volume is of a failed attempt; the transcendental vision of the first few *Rimas* is quickly spent and the poems gravitate towards a straightforward account of thwarted love couched in ordinary language. Bécquer's confused awareness of the constrictive outwardness of the poetry of his times was never translated into a fully-fledged symbolist theory,[11] although his example was an inspiration to *fin-de-siècle* modernists for whom the collapse of realism revealed the significance of his experiments.

By the 1890s the subjective revolution in literature brought by romanticism had hardly affected Spain. When it came, with modernism, it released a flood of pent-up talent. Spain, which had produced only two writers of European stature between 1650 and 1890 (Galdós and Alas), now suddenly saw the appearance in print, between about 1890 and 1905, of five major writers (Unamuno, Valle-Inclán, Juan Ramón Jiménez, Gabriel Miró, Antonio Machado) whose best work, though often poorly translated or not translated at all, is an important contribution to European literature. There is a case for adding the names of Azorín and Pío Baroja to this list. Numerous brilliant writers followed in rapid succession, including Pérez de Ayala, Gómez de la Serna, García Lorca, Rafael Alberti, Jorge Guillén, Luis Cernuda and Miguel Hernández. The reputation of some of these writers has been consolidated outside Spain. At least two of them, Gabriel Miró and Ramón del Valle-Inclán, are surely among Europe's finest novelists. The thirty years after 1900 were amazingly fertile for Spanish literature, and this remarkable renaissance came about because writers were at last freed, by the fall of the dominant realist aesthetic, from the canons of popularity and intelligibility imposed by two centuries of anti-aestheticism. In the process, of course, they also lost much of their potential readership: many of their works are still accessible only to a highly literate elite. But in a country like the Spain of the 1920s and 1930s, literature must constantly run ahead of any potential mass readership if authors are to be freed from the stylistic, linguistic, conceptual and moral constraints imposed by those who would make existing popular tastes into literary universals.

Modernism achieved the liberation of Spanish writers from moral, political or patriotic accountability to a philistine readership. A digression is necessary however, because the term 'modernism' is almost unknown in Spanish studies. Since the present argument about politics and literature in Spain rests on the view that modernism is the living tradition in twentieth-century Spanish literature, a few remarks about its identity seem appropriate.

I take modernism to mean the rejection of realism and the move towards non-representationalism which is common to such movements as impressionism, cubism, futurism, symbolism, imagism, vorticism, Dadaism and surrealism in the literature and art of Europe in the period 1890 to 1930, and to the corresponding Spanish movements *modernismo*, *creacionismo*, *ultraísmo*, *gongorismo* and *surrealismo* and other experimental innovations such as the *greguerías* of Gómez de la Serna, Unamuno's *nivola*, *perspectivismo*, Valle's *esperpento* technique and other non-realist devices.[12]

Of the outstanding authors of the period 1895 to 1936 all, except Baroja and Blasco Ibáñez, based their major works on a spirit of rebellion against social realism. This is obviously true of *modernistas* such as Jiménez, Villaespesa and Manuel Machado, and of *avant-*

garde writers such as Gómez de la Serna, Benjamín Jarnés, Francisco Ayala, Pérez de Ayala, Guillén, Lorca, Alberti and Cernuda (at least in his early poems), Miguel Hernández and others. But it is also true of other writers, the 'modernity' of whose formal experiments is often overlooked—Unamuno, 'Azorín', Antonio Machado and Valle-Inclán. In the first three cases this is because the writers are usually thought of as belonging to another, separate literary movement defined by an allegedly distinctive content, the so-called 'Generation of '98', a term which refers to no specific literary technique, style or device, and which has no counterpart elsewhere in European literary studies.[13] Unamuno rejected realism and experimented with formal devices analogous, in the case of his novel *Niebla* (1914), to Pirandello's treatment of realism in *Six Characters in Search of an Author*. Azorín made bold experiments in non-realist novel writing in works such as *Doña Inés* (1925), *Félix Vargas* (1928), *Superrealismo* (1929). If Brecht is counted as a modernist, then Valle-Inclán's brilliant treatment of the problems of realism (see Chapter Four) qualifies him also for consideration as a major European modernist. Since modernism is a description of techniques, it follows that some works of a single writer may embody more modernist techniques than others. Some authors, such as Machado and Cernuda, started in modernism but evolved away from it, back towards realism in Machado's case. Others, Pérez de Ayala and Unamuno for instance, began in the realist tradition but rejected it for modernist experiments. Others, such as Alberti (and to some extent Lorca), fluctuated in their attitude towards modernist devices, usually according to the state of their political enthusiasms.

The Spanish modernists were bold experimenters indeed. Some went as far as any comparable European writers with technical innovations such as non-linear plots, parallel dialogue, stream-of-consciousness, semi-automatic writing, cinematographic effects, allegory, mythical substructures, symbolic form, distancing techniques and so on. The overall effect of these thirty years of experimentation was to create a literary language as remote from everyday speech as had been the ornate diction of the Baroque writers. It does not always follow that these linguistic and formal innovators were also political elitists. Some aligned themselves with progressive movements, others with conservative ones, and several changed sides. Nevertheless, their work is the product of a self-conscious elite of artists not primarily concerned with the immediate effects of their writing on Spanish political or social life. This is perhaps incongruous in the fraught situation of Spanish politics in those years: there is something of Nero's fiddling about most of Spanish literature in that period.

Chapter Two

Modernism, Politics and the Critics

The Fate of Spanish Modernism

The literary achievement of the Spanish modernists was extraordinary, but it was curiously flawed. Spanish modernism never produced an accompanying body of justificatory critical writing which might have consolidated its gains over realism: to this extent it was prey to its own anti-intellectualism. No twentieth-century Spanish author wrote critical essays even remotely comparable with those of Eliot, Yeats or Brecht. None of the modernists, in particular, seem to have been able or willing to articulate clearly the theoretical premises of his work. In fact only those writers with misgivings about modern literature—Unamuno, Antonio Machado, Luis Cernuda—were fertile in critical arguments. No Spanish critic, not even Dámaso Alonso (see below), ever managed firmly to ground modernist techniques on the findings of some branch of critical, historical or extra-literary research such as the works of Freud, Jung or Frazer, Eliot's dissociation of sensibility, or the ideas of Hulme, Fenollosa, Bergson and others. In this vulnerable critical state, Spanish modernism was an easy prey to politicized critics who either championed it as the literature of a new anti-democratic aristocracy, or rejected it on the grounds that it was out of touch with popular life or enshrined bourgeois individualism.

It is not impossible to imagine a politically committed literature which would be rich and complex, and would not contain a simplified caricature of human nature expressed in a parody of 'popular' language. Such literature would either presuppose a highly literate population, or would be addressed to an educated elite responsive to sophisticated techniques. In an age of democratic politics, right- or left-wing, political literature is bound to be directed at an imagined mass readership and is thus usually written in kinds of language assumed to be accessible to a large public. In practice this has often meant writing at the level of traditional expectation about literature, in well-tried forms (ballads, melodrama, novels of suspense) and in language supposed to reflect normal conversation.

There are other constraints working on committed literature, though they are not always observed—particularly in Spain. Politically committed literature ought logically so to present human problems as to show how they arose from political circumstances; and it ought to show how they can be solved by new political choices. This is a reasonable thing to ask of a political vision, and it involves a necessary optimism about man's perfectibility. Political literature must contain the assumption that by reform, revolution or calculated inaction, institutions can be made to conform to what the writer calls Reason.

The point that politically committed literature must embody a belief in the usefulness of political action may seem tautological, but it is a reminder that merely describing and denouncing social conditions does not make a work 'committed'. Such writing may make the reader decide to commit himself, in the same way that a visit to Belgravia or shantytown may do so; but the commitment need not be in the writing itself. Social realism is the obvious (but not the only) technique of writers concerned with political questions, and there are special reasons, of which more later, why social realism should have become the slogan of many Spanish writers. But a number of Spanish authors (e.g. Baroja and perhaps Leopoldo Alas), have technically been realists, while their despair about their compatriots' capacity for self-improvement makes their work anything but politically committed. If a writer attributes his country's plight to congenital defects of temperament, to climate, race or to the gloomy conclusion that it is merely an acute instance of a human condition everywhere tragic and absurd, then he is likely to present his nation's politics as further examples of the general hopelessness, not as a potential remedy. Such gloom by no means precludes detailed and compassionate analyses of social conditions; but the resulting 'realism' is not necessarily a radical confrontation with those conditions. The fact that much post-Civil War critical writing in Spain seems to assume the contrary—i.e. that realism and commitment are the same thing—had many consequences for Spanish literature in the 1950s and 1960s.

This problem of the relationship between commitment and realism is most relevant to the development of the post-Civil War novel, although it bears on all genres. The problem of the effect of political commitment on literary language is best studied in the genre which suffered most from theorizing about commitment: poetry. But everywhere the recurrent theme has been that realism is the technique of humanist, popular or national writers, as opposed to the anti-realism of 'bourgeois', 'undemocratic' or 'elitist' literature. The implications of this idea have been far-reaching.

The zenith of modernist aestheticism coincided, significantly enough, with the nadir of progressive hopes under Primo de Rivera's military dictatorship from 1923 to 1930—a coincidence exploited by at least one astute Fascist critic to show how the arts flourish best under despotism.[1] As hopes grew after 1928 of radical changes following the fall of the dictatorship and monarchy, there was an inevitable tendency to judge literature by the degree to which it reflected the new, liberal or left-wing political enthusiasm. In fact, whereas in Britain the rejection of *fin-de-siècle* and Georgian aestheticism was made from a complex of positions—appeals to tradition, radical humanism, religion, 'realized Life' and the example of older literatures—critical debate in Spain about aestheticism and, in fact, about all modernism, has since before 1930 been bogged down in politics. By the mid-1930s Spanish criticism was well on the way to returning to pre-modernist ideas about the social responsibility of artists and the moral advantages of realism, and authoritative complaints were being heard that modernism was corrupt with aristocratic or bourgeois aloofness.

Ortega y Gasset and the Politicization of Modernism

This is not surprising when one considers the prestige and influence of José Ortega y Gasset. Spain is almost unique in having produced a strikingly political *defence* of modernism from an anti-democratic standpoint. The impact of Ortega's *The Dehumanization of Art* (*La deshumanización del arte*)[2] on subsequent Spanish arguments about the relationship between literature and politics has been far-reaching. Ortega has often been denounced as a Fascist. His politics later evolved, but there is no doubt that in the 1920s he was still under the influence of the extreme right-wing theories he had learnt from his German professors. His best-known work, *The Revolt of the Masses* (*La rebelión de las masas*, 1930), diagnoses the sickness of modern Europe as the levelling effects of democracy; his impractical solutions are the restoration of a hierarchy of 'excellence' in society and the exclusion of 'the masses' from decision making.

This is something less than Fascism in a strict sense. Ortega's theories contain none of the racialism or imperialist fantasies of the Fascists: he was inspired by nostalgia for the French *ancien régime*. The message of *La rebelión de las masas* can be read as much as a rejection of political intervention by low-bred generals as of Socialist policies. He later expressed great aversion to the collectivization of life under Nazism, and he called himself a liberal. Nevertheless, his political stance has usually been taken by left-wing and democratic critics as in some sense proto-Fascist, and it is against this background that one must interpret reactions to his ideas.

Ortega's arguments about modernism are most significant. He saw the elitism of the modern arts as socially divisive, and since he abhorred solidarity and collectivism welcomed this divisiveness.

In *La deshumanización del arte* he argues that the abstraction and syntactic and imagistic complexity of modern art and literature indicate a conscious rejection of mass taste by the artistic elite, and so demonstrate a will to reintroduce a hierarchy of cultural values in a world corrupted by ideas about the superiority of majority taste:

> A mi juicio, lo característico del arte nuevo, 'desde el punto de vista sociológico', es que divide al público en estas dos clases de hombres: los que lo entienden y los que no lo entienden. (p. 4)
> (*In my view, the characteristic of the new art from 'a sociological point of view', is that it divides the public into two types: those that understand it and those who do not.*)

Ortega finds this separation fundamental: the first group 'possesses an organ of the understanding not possessed by the others, they are two varieties of the human species' (ibid). The perplexing difficulty of the modern arts, from Debussy and Mallarmé on, will enable the 'minority' to become a self-conscious aristocratic elite:

> La música de Stravinsky o el drama de Pirandello tienen la eficacia de obligar (a la masa) a reconocerse como lo que es, como 'sólo pueblo', mero ingrediente, entre otros, de la estructura social, inerte materia del proceso histórico, factor secundario del cosmos espiritual. Por otra parte, el arte joven contribuye también a que los 'mejores' se conozcan y reconozcan entre el gris de la muchedumbre y aprendan su misión, que consiste en ser pocos y tener que combatir contra los muchos.
>
> Se acerca el tiempo en que la sociedad, desde la política al arte, volverá a organizarse, según es debido, en dos órdenes o rangos:

el de los hombres egregios y el de los hombres vulgares. (p. 5)
*(Stravinsky's music or Pirandello's drama are useful in so far as they
oblige the masses to recognize themselves for what they are, as 'simply
the common people', a mere ingredient among others in the social
structure, inert matter in the historical process, a secondary factor in
the spiritual cosmos. The young arts, moreover, assist the 'superior' to
know and recognise one another amidst the grey of the multitudes, and
to learn their mission, which consists in being few in number and
having to struggle against the many.*

*A time is drawing near when, from politics to art, society will once
again be organized, as it must be, into two ranks or orders: that of the
men of excellence and that of ordinary men.)*

Ortega's examples of this 'young art' are Debussy, Stravinsky,
Pirandello, Proust, Mallarmé, Joyce, Gómez de la Serna, Giraudoux,
Dadaism and the *ultraísta* movement: in short, modernism. The
significance of his remarks can hardly be overstressed. With him,
debate about the relationship between literature and public life takes
an important step. He identifies realism as 'always' (p. 10) the favourite
artistic technique of the ordinary masses. Realism reached its apogee
in the nineteenth century, when artists 'always proceeded too
impurely' by reducing strictly aesthetic elements to a minimum and
composing their works almost entirely 'on the fiction of human
realities ... Beethoven and Wagner, Chateaubriand and Zola were
realists' (p. 10). The new sensibility involves a systematic elimination
of 'the human' from the arts. The 'imperative demand for exclusive
realism' which Ortega takes to have characterized nineteenth-century
art and literature is a 'monstrosity' in aesthetic evolution. 'Since
Debussy, we can listen to music serenely without intoxication (*embria-
guez*) or weeping' (p. 29). Since the time of Mallarmé there has been
a systematic demarcation between art and ordinary life, a sort of
'taboo' operating against the representation of human things.
Metaphors, so characteristic of modern literature, are themselves
indicative of this taboo, of a systematic refusal to call things by their
ordinary name (pp. 33–4). So strong is the modern rejection of the
idea of art and literature having any emotional, social or political
function, that the modern arts no longer believe in their own seriousness. 'For many of the new generation the new art is a thing
without ultimate purpose' (*sin trascendencia*) (p. 18). Previously the
arts have been viewed as solemn manifestations of human spirituality,

but they are now appearing more like a 'sport' at the 'periphery' of human affairs. Ortega takes this frivolity as indicative of the essential modesty of modern art, of its aspiration to be valued only on its own terms.

Ortega's *La deshumanización* must be read in the context of his general dislike of democracy. Despite his claims to critical neutrality, it is clear that he welcomes what he supposes to be the anti-democratic intention of modernism, its effect of imposing ranks and hierarchies on the shapeless mob of modern society: the creation of obscure art and literature will put barriers between the 'aristocracy' and the masses. This argument is an unfortunate development. Scarcely had the great innovatory movements of modernism got under way in Spain but they were encumbered by the patronage of this enemy of human equality and exasperating snob.

It seems to me that few Spanish writers and critics, however hostile to Ortega's motives, have ever really questioned his conclusions. The theme of 'dehumanization' runs as a leitmotif through much subsequent Spanish argument about the development of twentieth-century literature. Ortega politicized modernism: he identified it as the literature of a 'natural' ruling class which hates democracy. The aura of political suspectness surrounding any Spanish literature of imagistic or syntactic complexity has never since been dispelled.

Modernism and the Left in Spain

Given this basic acceptance of Ortega's terms, the left-wing position on modernism is predictable: the irrationalism and subjectivism of modernism reflect a class position. This is the view of the pre-Civil War critic José Díaz. For him, the success of 'formalist literatures' is a result of a reactionary conspiracy:

> Es indudable que el éxito de las literaturas formales constituye la prueba más convincente de la liquidación de un sistema social. Las presuntuosas literaturas de vanguardia no han tenido otra misión en la historia de nuestro siglo que anunciar el último vagido del siglo XIX. ¡Ellas que se creían matrices del futuro! . . . El vanguardismo literario es tan reaccionario en política como cualquiera de esos trogloditas de que habla Unamuno refiriéndose a los conservadores españoles.[3]

(There can be no doubt that the success of formal literatures provides the most convincing proof of the collapse of a social system. In the history of our century, the presumptuous literatures of the avant garde have had only one function: that of uttering the dying gasp of the nineteenth century. They who imagined themselves to be the womb of the future! ... The avant garde *in literature is as reactionary in politics as any of those troglodites Unamuno refers to when speaking of the Spanish conservatives.)*

Díaz has a number of suggestive ideas. He echoes Ortega's language by declaring that Soviet literature represents a 'return to the human' (*una vuelta a lo humano*). He takes the aesthetics of the *avant garde* to be a kind of updated neo-classicism. To replace it he advocates a return to precisely the kind of romantic concern with 'human feelings' that Ortega abhors. He goes so far as to suggest that the renewed interest in Baroque poetry which followed Dámaso Alonso's revaluation of Luis de Góngora in 1927 is a literary expression of a general reactionary revival of 'neo-Catholic' politics (*El nuevo romanticismo* p. 80).

The concession that the *avant-garde* writer can nevertheless be politically progressive does not seem to have been made by Marxist or left-wing critics until after the Civil War. A clear expression of the idea is found in José María Castellet's work. Castellet was a champion of the social realist movement of the 1950s and 1960s, and his critical theories are very reminiscent of Ortega's—although the political commitment is of course the reverse. In the introduction to his anthology of twentieth-century Spanish poetry,[4] he claims to discern a steady evolution of modern poetry away from the 'dehumanized' subjectivism of symbolism and the *avant garde*, towards a socially orientated poetry written in colloquial language. This return to 'realism' is seen as a renewed awareness on the part of poets of the modern writer's re-commitment to the progressive movement after an escapist interlude. The argument is applied to European poetry in general in a later work in Catalan. Here, he acknowledges *avant-garde* writing as a revolt against the oppressive realities of capitalism but notes that this revolt paradoxically involves a confirmation of that reality:

L'escriptor creu trobar en l'exercici del seu art noves formes que alliberen l'obra literària de la subjecció a la realitat quotidiana; i així, doncs, creu que ateny un grau màxim de llibertat, accentuat en el camp poètic, pel deseiximent no sols de la realitat, sinó de les

convencions poètiques en ús; tanmateix realitza un doble acte de submissió: en primer lloc perquè ha acceptat la falsa alternativa que les classes dirigents li proposaven i, en segon lloc, perquè la seva acceptació duu automàticament la subjecció del seu art a unes condicions que impliquen la pèrdua del seu públic.[5]
(*The writer thinks he discovers in practising his art new forms which liberate the literary work from subjection to everyday reality; thus he imagines that he is achieving a maximum of freedom especially in the poetic field, by freeing himself not only from reality but from standard poetic conventions. In fact he is performing a double act of submission: first because he has accepted the false alternative offered him by the ruling classes; secondly because his acceptance automatically leads to subjection of his art to conditions which imply the loss of his audience.*)

Antonio Machado. Radical Liberalism and Spanish Modernism

Castellet is a post-War critic. José Díaz's ideas seem to have had little impact. The major left-wing critical reaction to modernism came from Antonio Machado (1875–1936), the most popular poet of modern Spain.[6] He must share responsibility with Ortega for establishing the critical principle that modernism is an expression of bourgeois individualism.

Machado's early poetry is very much part of the symbolist tradition, and its subjectivism verges on an unhealthy solipsism. Despite this, he had from the start been critical of the formalism of Spanish *modernista* poetry of the 1890s, and even his earliest verse can be read as a series of attempts to overcome some of the early modernists' obsession with metrical and rhythmical effects. A theme of his poetry which grows in importance is also a longing to escape from the enclosed world of his own psyche (cf. poems such as 'La fuente'), an urge which conflicts with the charms of dream and memory. His second collection of poems, *Campos de Castilla* (composed between 1907 and 1917), celebrates this escape and represents a significant departure from the modernist tradition. In a number of poems the themes are public ones: Spain's imperial history and present decline, the economic and cultural problems of modern Spain, the chances of national regeneration. The poems revert to earlier formal traditions. Machado even tries his hand at a genre which has tempted several Spanish poets with populist social consciences: the narrative ballad or *romance* ('Tierra de Alvargonzález').

After 1917 Machado's interests turned more and more to philosophical and critical questions. His scattered remarks on these matters had some impact in their day, but it is more probable, as Castellet says,[7] that Machado's critical theories became widespread only in the 1950s, when they were quoted as an authoritative left-wing rejection of modernism. Machado achieved almost legendary fame as a propagandist for the Republican cause in the Civil War, and died in a refugee camp after fleeing from Nationalist troops in 1939. Although never a Marxist, he was obviously sympathetic to the left-wing and pro-Communist forces within the Republic. It is difficult to assess his views on Socialism. His ideas about literature and culture are those of a Socialist, but he seems to have had little idea of the political or economic bases of Socialism.[8]

A fact that is generally overlooked is that like the other left-wing critics quoted, Machado in fact endorses Ortega's analysis of modernism without reservation, even though his political position is the reverse of Ortega's:

> Cuantos seguimos con alguna curiosidad el movimiento literario moderno, pudiéramos señalar la eclosión de múltiples escuelas ... que todas ellas tuvieron, al fin, un denominador común: guerra a la razón y al sentimiento, es decir a las dos formas de comunión humana.[9]
>
> (*Those of us who follow the modern literary movement with some curiosity could point to the emergence of many schools ... whose common denominator is ultimately war on reason and feeling—the two forms of human communion.*)

Although imprecise about the components of the 'modern literary movement', it is clear that he is referring to modernism. There is much confusion in Machado's notes about the exact deficiencies of modernism. He condemns it both for 'intellectualism' and for irrationalism, both for 'subjectivism' and for lack of real inwardness or intimacy. However, this quotation contains the main features of the argument: belief in universal human Reason, which derives from Plato, and belief in love and human dialogue, originating in the teachings of Christ, are the preconditions for successful human communication. 'Modern literature' denies both and is therefore socially divisive—precisely, of course, the aspect of modernism which

Ortega admired. Machado accuses modern literature of abandoning the business of communication and goes further than Ortega by linking this anti-humanism with the romantic movement itself. Although 'romantic individualism' did not exclude universality, it lost a 'sense of proportion' by rejecting belief in anything outside the individual subject. Romantic individualism, Machado argues, makes the mistake of believing that what is individual in human beings is 'inexpressible in generic terms', so that in the later stages of romanticism writers renounce the ideal of communication completely (*Los complementarios* 114–15).

The crux of the matter for Machado is the question of 'generic' language, and here he strikes a telling blow against modernism. Machado is hostile to the experimental language of modern literature. He particularly distrusts the metaphorical richness of modern poetry which he finds gratuitous: 'Good poets are sparing in the use of metaphor' (p. 34). According to Machado, a characteristic of great poets (he specifies Homer) is a deliberate use of 'generic' language (*lenguaje genérico*): 'When Homer says "the hollow bark" he is not describing any specific boat but simply giving a definition of a boat and a viewpoint from which to see boats.' When modern art does away with 'defining adjectives or the generic scheme of things in order to give us the lived sensation of a unique object or the fleeting impression in a particular soul (*un alma singular*), it makes too much of a sacrifice ... Let us not forget that generic images have their aesthetic value' (pp. 37–8). Poets must remember that language is a social creation belonging to the 'world of other selves', and this imposes limits on their private creativity. Consequently, Machado concludes, all poetry is a type of dialogue in which the form of the final poem is a compromise negotiated between author and reader: the discovery of the right expression for both poet and his fellow men.

Machado explicitly identifies the subjectivism of romanticism with *laissez-faire* capitalism.[10] For a solution to the problem, however, he vacillates (characteristically) between advocating political revolution and philosophical changes. In an article on Soviet Russia and the future of literature he speculates on the possibility of a new poetry based on fraternity, for which 'a communist faith will be necessary' (*será necesaria una fe comunista*).[11] This might bring about a triumph of realism in both the literary and philosophical sense. Elsewhere he argues that the 'subjective idealism' which underlies most romantic and post-romantic literature, must be replaced by a new radical distinction between subject and object. Men must acquire a new awareness of what Machado calls the 'essential heterogeneity of being' (*la esencial heterogeneidad del ser*), i.e. of the fact that reality consists of a plurality of independent and autonomous subjects and objects which do not owe their existence to our perception of them:

> El yo egolátrico del ayer aparece hoy más humilde ante las cosas. Ellas están ahí y nadie ha probado que las engendre yo cuando las veo. (p. 127)

> (*The self-centred ego of yesterday nowadays shows itself as more humble in the presence of things. Things are there and no one has proved that I create them when I see them.*)

This defence of a fresh awareness of 'things' had important implications for post-War poetry and novels, and we shall return to the subject.[12]

Some Fascist reactions to Modernism

In view of the left's distrust of modernism as an elitist phenomenon, it might be expected that Fascist critics would welcome it, as Ortega did, as the appropriate literature for a hierarchical society. Had Fascists appropriated modernism as their literature, the history of post-War Spanish literature would have been very different, although official recognition of pre-Civil War literature by the new regime would have damned it for ever in the eyes of the opposition.

Despite Ortega's defence of the 'elitism' of modernism's convoluted syntax and imagery, Fascist critics seem to have endorsed the views of Antonio Machado and the left: they diagnose the subjectivism and impenetrability of modernism as an expression of liberal individualism, and condemn it. It may be that the points at which their arguments coincide with Machado's and Díaz's views represent the common ground in the anti-modernist campaign of the politicized critics.

The point is worth labouring. Distrust of modernism was by no means confined to humanist critics. The sides taken in this controversy are not those of 'reaction' versus 'progress', but of individualism versus collectivism. What Fascists and left-wing critics share is a belief in the need for a common culture to replace the fragmented individualism of the liberal age. The road to this common goal is, of course, widely different in each case: Fascist collectivism is based on common racial and national interests, and the left envisage a homogeneous culture based on a single class or on the *pueblo*. But neither Fascists nor Socialists admitted the type of individualism which Ortega thought was reflected in the fanciful subjectivism of modernism. In fact the basic difference between Ortega and the Fascists is that the former's attack on democracy is based on a belief that democracy threatens individualism. The Fascists took the opposite view that individualism and democracy are basically evil.

This argument may well offend sympathizers with the post-Civil War democratic movement in Spain, which has traditionally held Machado's ideas to be pinnacles of liberal humanist achievement. They obviously are, and no criticism of his motives is here implied. Yet the convergence between his and Fascist critical theories is instructive. Although the left and extreme right have literally been mortal enemies in Spain, their critical premises have been strangely similar at a deeper level.

The most coherent Spanish Fascist theory of art and literature is contained in Giménez Caballero's *Arte y estado*.[13] Giménez Caballero was initially a modernist. He published a surrealistic work in 1928, *Yo inspector de alcantarillas*, and in 1927 helped to found an *avant-garde* review, *La Gaceta Literaria*. After a visit to Mussolini's Rome in 1928 his sympathies warmed to Fascism, and he became a fanatical supporter of the cause after the fall of the Spanish Monarchy. He contributed to Fascist publications such as *La Conquista del Estado*, *El Fascio*, *Falange Española* and *Arriba*. His *Genio de España* (1932) was widely read by Nationalists during the Civil War, and his enthusiasms survived the conflict to appear in several semi-official post-War Fascist publications such as *Jerarquía*, *Vértice* and *Fantasía*.

Arte y estado is written in the high-flown poetastry peculiar to Fascism. The argument is interesting, however, and his knowledge of contemporary artistic movements is creditable. Essentially he demands a 'heroic' art form for the New State which will draw on some aspects of modernism, notably on Le Corbusier in architecture and on early post-Revolutionary Soviet art. More interesting is his critique of 'subjectivism'. He rejects the artistic forms of liberalism more vigorously than those of Communism; he admires the latter as inspired by an authoritarian system (p. 26). Symptomatic of the crisis of 'liberal humanist civilization' is the elitism of the modern arts, and

29

the triumph of 'Jewish' subjective ideologies such as Bergsonism and that of Freud—the latter being especially evident in surrealism (p. 36). Minority art has always been alien to Spain, and Spanish artists and writers have traditionally cultivated that element of their inspiration which comes not from individual acts of imagination, but from 'tradition' (p. 36). Art is great to the extent to which it embodies collective feelings, so that nationalistic doggerel is worth more than the 'delicate outpourings of French purism (*los finos vertederos del purismo francés*) in miniature editions' (p. 205).

The anti-Semitism apart, the tendency of the argument is not unlike Machado's complaint against modern subjectivism. Giménez Caballero's proposed remedies are more disconcerting. Fascism will abolish liberalism and democracy and correct subjective excesses (p. 88). Secular 'monasteries' of uniformed and disciplined artists will replace the 'Bohemian individualism' of modern writing. A Ministry for Propaganda and Culture, modelled on Goebbels' equivalent and headed by Giménez himself, will organize artistic production. As a model, Giménez Caballero advocates Soviet literature—with the reservation that its content must be Christian and 'spiritual'.

José María Pemán, at that time a fanatical monarchist with Fascist sympathies, put forward rather similar anti-modernist arguments in the preface to his vulgar anti-Semitic tract, *Poema de la bestia y del ángel*.[14] Pemán condemns the 'dehumanized' subjectivism of modern poetry, a dehumanization which, like Ortega, he dates from the time of Mallarmé (p. 10). Divorced from 'reality', the modern poet indulges in absurd licence,

> encerrado dentro de sí mismo, construyendo su poema de puras intuiciones sin objeto externo. . . . Para Santo Tomás, que miraba hacia fuera y que no creía que en su intelecto hubiera nada que primero no hubiera estado en los sentidos, el mar tenía que ser necesariamente azul. Pero para el poeta puro que todo lo elabora dentro de la autonomía de su espíritu, bien podía haber un mar amarillo, poblado, si es preciso, de pájaros o de gacelas. (p. 12)
> (*enclosed within himself, building his poem from pure intuitions without an external object . . . For St Thomas, who looked outwards and did not believe that his intellect contained anything but had first been in his senses, the sea had to be blue. But for the pure poet who concocts everything from within the autonomy of his mind, there could well be a yellow sea, inhabited if necessary by birds or gazelles.*)

Pemán goes on to complain that 'pure poetry' has evolved an expressive language without relating it to an external object. This object, he argues, should have been the external world (cf. Machado's 'return to objectivity'), and also God. Future poets will abandon such wayward subjectivism and write about 'universals like Nature, Heaven and Hell'. An admirable genre for such work will be the epic, which expresses a collective rather than a personal world picture (p. 15).

Concluding Remarks: Modern Spanish Literature and the Critics

Although the politics of all these critics differ widely there are obvious common themes in their arguments. All (except of course Ortega, the sole admirer of modernism), defend popular forms against the innovations of modern writers, and all consider that great literature is basically an expression of a period of history rather than of a moment in an individual's experience. All tend to object not so much to the work of their political opponents right or left, as to writing which smacks of individualist elitism, or cosmopolitan or minority tastes. Both right- and left-wing critics reject the 'idealism' underlying modernism and recommend traditional or colloquial forms as models, with a strong bias towards realism.

In fact, the arguments examined so far add little to nineteenth-century notions about the national or popular basis of great literature. The only important addition to Núñez de Arce's analysis of the function of realism is Ortega's idea that realism is the literary mode of a specific social *class*. All the critics quoted are unanimous in identifying modernism as the literature of writers dissociated from ordinary life—whether this is the life of the *pueblo* (the liberal-democratic ideal) or of the proletariat (the Socialist ideal) or of the 'Nation' (the ideal of the right).

Nor do these arguments simply bear on *avant-garde* extravagances. They are applied, vaguely, to 'modern' writing in general; and, in the absence of any clear indications on the critics' part, we must assume that 'elitism' is characteristic of the entire artistic tradition which resuscitated Spanish poetry after 1900: imagism, *modernismo*, *gongorismo*, *ultraísmo* and surrealism, the whole exploration of language and the inner world which produced the best of Jiménez, Lorca,

Alberti, Guillén (whom Machado singles out for criticism) and many others. Detailed analyses of actual texts are rarely found in the critical arguments so far summarized. But the general strictures applied to the 'cult of the metaphor', 'subjectivism' and 'pure poetry' strike at the heart of the whole modernist literary movement. Even the critic who had done most to revive interest in Baroque poetry, Dámaso Alonso, repudiated the achievement of modernist poets:

> Si he acompañado a esta generación como crítico, apenas como poeta. Las doctrinas estéticas de hacia 1927, que para otros fueron tan estimables, a mí me resultaron heladoras de todo impulso creativo. Para expresarme con libertad necesité la terible sacudida de la guerra española.[15]
>
> (If I accompanied this generation (i.e. that of Lorca, Alberti, Guillén and other modernists) as a critic, I have scarcely done so as a poet. The aesthetic doctrines of around 1927, so much appreciated by others, actually chilled any kind of creative impulse in me. To express myself freely I needed the terrible shock of the Spanish War.)

It is a terrible comment on the fervour of his distrust of 'modern' poetry that Antonio Machado felt that a slight benefit from the Spanish Civil War would be the destruction of the 'cult of the image':

> La guerra, como tema obligado, con su terrible urgencia apasionante, va apartando a nuestros poetas del fetichismo de las imágenes.[16]
>
> (The War, as an obligatory topic, with its terrible, passion-generating urgency, is distracting our poets from the fetichism of imagery.)

The fruits of this mounting distrust of experimental writing were harvested in the dismal years following General Franco's victory in 1939.

Chapter Three

Modernist Poetry and Politics, 1936–65

'La consideración de la vida humana como solidaridad, que sirve de base a buena parte de las letras actuales, la correlativa disminución del lirismo, suplantado por directrices semi-narrativas, parecen indicar que el individualismo artístico está a punto de extinguirse.'

(Carlos Bousoño, 1958)

('The idea of human life as solidarity, which underlies much of contemporary literature, and the corresponding decline of lyricism which is being replaced by semi-narrative principles, seem to indicate that artistic individualism is on the verge of extinction.')

Modern Spanish Poetry, Politics and the Civil War

The Spanish Civil War was a catastrophe for Spanish poetry as it was for every kind of cultural activity. Of the major pre-Civil War poets, Lorca was murdered, Unamuno died under house arrest for outspoken remarks about the Fascist cause; Miguel Hernández perished in a Fascist prison in 1942; Rafael Alberti, Jorge Guillén, Luis Cernuda, Juan Ramón Jiménez and Antonio Machado went into exile—the last to die shortly after crossing the French frontier. Scarcely a single major poet remained in Spain.

This annihilation of a generation of poets might in itself explain the death of the modernist tradition in Spanish poetry and account for the dramatic difference between pre- and post-Civil War poetry. But it cannot be the only reason. The diction and forms of modernism could have been continued either by the victorious right or the defeated left. The pious Catholic poets who stepped with undeserved ease into the vacuum left by their predecessors could have continued their formal experiments: Pound, Eliot and Yeats were hardly liberals or left-wing, yet their conservatism did not extend to a rejection of modernist

33

techniques. The example of Neruda who, despite his declared aversion to 'pure' poetry incorporated much of modernism into his Socialist poetry, indicates how the tradition of Lorca, Alberti and others could have been continued by the left. There is no intrinsic quality in pre-War modernism which explains its rejection by post-War poets in Spain.

Yet modernist poetry really only survived in exile, like the Spanish liberal tradition with which it had become associated. Jiménez, Jorge Guillén, Luis Cernuda[1] and Rafael Alberti continued to write modernist poetry, though whether any of them (except Jiménez) can be said to have perfected his art in exile seems to me doubtful. Inside Spain a different series of poetic formulas was tried, all of them based to a greater or lesser extent on models or aesthetic theories from much earlier periods of Spanish poetry. I propose in this chapter to consider mainly the work of left-wing poets who eventually rejected the idea of artistic individualism.

The full force of systematic anti-modernism was not felt by Spanish poetry until after the Civil War. Caught out by the dramatic polarization of Spain and by the sudden prospect of a full-scale social revolution in the areas as yet unoccupied by Fascist troops, left-wing modernist poets in 1936 did not have the leisure to reflect on the artistic problems of revolutionary poetry. With no clear theories to hand about the formal problems of political poetry, they at best relied on some of the techniques of modernism they had learnt in calmer years, at worst jettisoned their aesthetic stock-in-trade in favour of crude ballads.

A striking feature of left-wing poetry from the Civil War period is the old-fashioned quality of its language and themes. The only formal precedents for a populist poetry sanctioned by Spanish tradition were the *romances*, the eight-syllable ballads of the Middle Ages so admired by patriotic romantics as the authentic literature of the Spanish people. Large quantities of political doggerel in *romance* metre were produced by anti-Fascist versifiers during the Civil War.[2] It is hard to believe that some of these versifiers were poets who had formed a common poetic movement with Lorca. The complete absence of any kind of poetic intensity in the War ballads of the modernist Emilio Prados is particularly striking, although Lorca in *Romancero gitano* (1928) had shown the potential of the *romance* in the hands of a modernist.

The use of the ballad for trench poetry points to another feature of

Spanish political poetry—its tendency to gravitate towards classical models. Left-wing poets organized homages to the seventeenth-century dramatist Lope de Vega, and Machado had been fascinated by medieval literature as a 'popular' literature. Right-wing poets, on the other hand, were tempted by early renaissance poets such as Garcilaso de la Vega, partly because his diction was still limpid and free of the 'intellectualism' of the Baroque and its historical associations with the decline of Spain, partly because Garcilaso, poet and imperial soldier, could serve as a model for the Fascists' new Spaniard.

As far as left-wing poetry is concerned, there is no doubt a deeper reason for the conventional language and tired patriotic rhetoric of War ballads. The majority of the poets were Communists or fellow travellers, and Communist policy was bound to find expression in traditional forms. A truly revolutionary vision might have created a Spanish Mayakovsky or some kind of futurist poetry similar to that written immediately after the Soviet revolution. But the Communist Party played down the social content of the anti-Fascist movement. From the start it declared that the issue in Spain was not the structure of Spanish society but the survival of liberal democracy threatened by 'foreign invaders' (Germans and Italians). It is not therefore surprising that Communist policies were endorsed by moderates and liberals, and inspired verse reminiscent of the liberal orators of the nineteenth century. A frequent historical reference used by Communist orators was, indeed, the patriotic uprising of the Spanish against the Napoleonic invasion, an uprising of ambiguous social and political content. Rooted, at least for rhetorical purposes, in patriotism and liberalism, the visionless programme of the Communists clothed itself in clichés—laments for the dead, denunciation of Moors and Germans, threnodies for patriotic heroes. The word 'Socialist' is rarely found.

Rafael Alberti

Rafael Alberti is a famous example of a modernist poet who turned Communist and devoted himself to writing propaganda. Alberti had been one of the boldest experimental writers of the 1920s. His work had been open to every kind of modernist influence, including cubism, *ultraísmo* and surrealism. He even attempted imitations of the Baroque poet Luis de Góngora. *Sobre los ángeles* (1927) exploits

35

surrealist imagery to produce one of those happy fusions of *avant-garde* verbal energy and emotional intensity which distinguishes pre-Civil War Spanish poetry. It was after this work that the fall of the monarchy and the prospects of social revolution inflamed Alberti with Socialist enthusiasms. In subsequent poems he appeared to repudiate the 'Gongorine marble of the shapes of his voice'[3] as he now called his earlier work.

Rafael Alberti's political poetry is extremely uneven. At points it falls back into conventional forms of a triteness not easily explicable in a poet whose verbal ingenuity had often been gratuitous. At others it incorporates modernist forms into propaganda poetry to produce poems of impressive power, at least compared with the 'social' poetry of the post-Civil War period. Of the poems like 'Colegio (S.J.)' there is little to say: an example shows how far such poems had jettisoned the technique of his modernist period. The description is of a Jesuit education:

> No es posible que vuelva este mismo paisaje,/que reconquiste ni por un momento su sueño embrutecido de moscas/formol y humo./No es posible otra vez este retrete sórdido de hábitos con eructos y sopa de tapioca./No es posible,/no quiero,/no es posible querer para vosotros la misma infancia y muerte.[4]
>
> *It's not possible for this same landscape to return/for it to regain even for a moment its dream/soiled with flies, and formol and smoke./It's not possible again this sordid lavatory of priests' clothes belches and tapioca soup./It isn't possible,/I don't want,/it's impossible to want the same childhood and death for all of you.*

Other poems stay closer to modernism, but rarely is the poetic charge of the earlier poems regained. Like the 'social' poets of the 1950s, Alberti seems to have come through the experience of War and Fascism with a deep distrust of his own poetic gift:

> Si no hubiera tantos males,/yo de mis coplas haría/torres de pavos reales./Pero a aquél lo están matando,/a éste lo están consumiendo/y a otro lo están enterrando./Por eso es hoy mi cantar/canto de pocas palabras . . ./y algunas están de más.[5]
>
> *(Were there not so many evils,/I'd make from my verse/towers of peacocks./But that man's being killed,/this one consumed,/that one buried./That's why my song today/is a song of scanty words . . ./and some of them too many.)*

In some of the political poems, Alberti's gift for effective images barely saves poems whose classical rhyme schemes and gusty rhetoric are reminiscent of nothing so much as the liberal oratory of early nineteenth-century demagogues such as Cienfuegos:

> Alba y ocaso, aurora y sol poniente,/fecha mortal y claro alumbramiento,/este día, gran día, inmenso día./Convulsa, ciega, temerariamente,/en un horror, en un sacudimiento,/alumbra España lo que al fin quería . . .[6]
>
> (*Dawn and dusk, sunrise and sunset,/fatal date and bright birth,/this day, great day, immense day./Convulsed, blind, rashly,/in a horror, in a shudder Spain/gives birth to what she willed* . . .)

Here the uncontrolled rhetoric contrasts strangely with the conventionally correct rhyme scheme.

It would be too much to expect poets to produce formal *tours de force* in mid-Civil War. The problem with Alberti is not so much the weaknesses of his political poetry, which is among the best of its kind in Spain, as the effects of this detour into propaganda on his other poetry. A poet capable of writing sonnets like 'A los derechos del hombre' ('To Human Rights'), (*Obras completas*, p. 774) has clearly lost some of his poetic insight. This poem, from *Poemas diversos* (1945–59), is occasional verse at its worst. Alberti was, after the War, quite capable of producing political verse to order, and something of this occasional quality sticks to nearly all his post-War poetry. He never regained the intensity and power of *Sobre los ángeles*, and his excursion into public oratory may well be the cause of this decline.

Miguel Hernández

Miguel Hernández's left-wing poetry shows how the techniques of modernism could be exploited for inspiring and durable political poems. The popularity of Hernández's poetry among anti-Franco Spaniards in the post-War years compares strikingly with a general lack of interest in the prosaic 'social poetry' of the same period—a telling point against the anti-modernist assumptions underlying 'social poetry'.

Miguel Hernández is an unusual case of a poet whose commitment to modernist language survived his political commitment. His work expresses every possible type of political attitude. In about five years

37

he went from detached neo-Baroque mannerism in works such as *Perito en lunas* (1933), through extreme clerical Fascism in the *Auto sacramental* described below and in such extraordinary 'Catholic' poems as *Primera lamentación de la carne*; to Communism in *Viento del pueblo* and *El hombre acecha*, and to a courageous resignation to defeat, imprisonment and fatal illness in *Romancero de ausencias*.

His clerical period is characterized by powerful imitations of seventeenth-century poetry full of rhetorical piety. A most extraordinary product of this Fascist period is an imitation of a Calderonian mystery play or *Auto sacramental*, *Quién te ha visto y quién te ve y sombra de lo que eres* (1934), a political allegory depicting the Fall as the subversion of God's *latifundio* by the five senses dressed in the red and black scarves of Anarchist revolutionaries. . . .

The Civil War inspired *Viento del pueblo* (1937) written while he was a political commissar for the Communist Party. It is a powerful volume which escapes the traps of populism, even though out of their context the poems have little real political content. Many consist of laments for the Republican dead, powerful but conventional. A number consist of denunciations of the violence of war, but again the theme and its treatment are held at a conventional level and lead to no real political conclusions. The most famous, however, has a savage strength which makes it one of the most vivid anti-Fascist poems of the War:

> Asturianos de braveza/vascos de piedra blindada,/valencianos de alegría/y castellanos de alma,/labrados como la tierra/y airosos como las alas;/andaluces de relámpago,/nacidos entre guitarras/y forjados en los yunques/torrenciales de las lágrimas;/gallegos de lluvia y calma,/catalanes de firmeza,/aragoneses de casta,/murcianos de dinamita/frutalmente propagada,/leoneses, navarros, dueños/del hambre, el sudor y el hacha,/reyes de la minería,/señores de la labranza,/hombres que entre las raíces,/como raíces gallardas,/vais de la vida a la muerte,/vais de la nada a la nada:/Yugos os quieren poner/gentes de la hierba mala . . .[7]
>
> *(Asturians of fury,/Basques of armoured stone,/Valencians of joy,/Castilians of soul,/fashioned like the earth,/as graceful as wings;/Andalusians like lightning,/born among guitars and forged on/torrential anvils of tears;/Galicians of rain and calm,/Catalans of firmness,/pure-blooded Aragonese,/Murcians of dynamite fruitfully*

thrown,/Leonese, Navarrese,/the owners of hunger, sweat and the axe,/kings of the mines,/lords of the ploughed land,/men who, among the roots,/like dashing roots,/go from nothingness/into nothing;/evil men are trying/to forge you a yoke ...)

Even when he is at his most political, Hernández tends to write about themes which he really understood: the rhythms of natural life. (He had been a shepherd, and was largely self-taught). His 'ode' to a Kharkov tractor factory (*Obras completas*, p. 225), written during an official visit to the USSR, reverts almost immediately to praise of the rhythms of nature and of sexual life. The poem has no real political content and could have been written of any busy car factory. The workshop is presented as a vast womb labouring to expel new vehicles, but the rather ridiculous analogy is concealed successfully by the sheer vigour of Hernández's imagery. Nevertheless, it is difficult to escape the conclusion that his poetry suffered a real loss in the formlessness and abstraction of his political verse. Modernism and political propaganda co-exist nervously in his left-wing poems, but he remains as an example of what left-wing verse could have been in Spain had anti-modernism not prevailed. Had he survived and circumstances been different, he might conceivably have become a Spanish Neruda.

Anti-Franco Poetry: the 'Poesía social' Movement

The Nationalist cause had generated intense Catholic, imperialist and anti-democratic excitement among the Spanish bourgeoisie, and this was expressed in the archaic, patriotic and religious poetry which had a brief vogue in the 1940s. This poetry, written mostly by Fascist or monarchist militants in semi-official magazines such as *Garcilaso*, was remote in content and language from the realities of post-War Spanish life. The poets invoked memories of the conquest of the Indies or God's bounty, but as they wrote Spain was in ruins and ravaged by famine and Europe on the verge of an even more destructive war. Such aloofness from reality was taken by left-wingers and humanists as further evidence for the critical theory which identified formalism and subjectivism with ruling-class ideology. So it was perhaps inevitable that post-Civil War liberal and left-wing poetry in Spain should go to opposite extremes of colloquialism and 'formlessness'.

39

The full effects of the left-wing repudiation of modernism were felt in the 'social poetry' movement of the 1950s and 1960s.[8] The adjective 'social' applied to literature in these years is a discreet euphemism for 'Socialist': all literature in Spain between 1939 and 1976 has been subject to official censorship, and words used in opposition literature under the Franco regime can rarely be taken simply at face value.

The 'social poetry' or *poesía social* movement dominated the years 1950 to 1965. The best-known poets of the movement are J. M. Caballero Bonald, Gabriel Celaya, Victoriano Crémer, Jose-María Gil de Biedma, Jesús López Pacheco, Blas de Otero and Ángel Valente. In general, the *poesía social* movement applied the criteria of 'humanized' poetry expounded in the works of Castellet and Antonio Machado described previously. The poems are characterized by an extreme flatness and colloquialism, an absence of all but the most conventional imagery, and much moralizing about abstractions such as 'Man', 'Love', 'Work' and so on. Such language is clearly in part a product of the censorship rules then prevailing. The Franco censorship was relatively mild compared, for example, with that of the USSR. Poets and other writers unlikely to find a large readership were permitted veiled circumlocutions about solidarity and humanism, and this explains the pious sermonizing of this poetry. But censorship by no means explains all its qualities. The complete absence in these poets' work of any acknowledgment of or positive allusion to the poetry of modernism is, of course, a direct effect of left-wing distrust of modernism. The *poesía social* movement was produced out of a poetic vacuum, without reference to any previous Spanish poetic tradition. Its forms, therefore, are taken direct from conversational language, and the poets clearly try to ensure that their verse retains the casual disjointedness of informal speech. *Poesía social* was not so much poetry as anti-poetry, and the poets deliberately ignored the achievement of modernist Spanish poetry.

Gabriel Celaya

The two most representative 'social poets' of the period are Gabriel Celaya and Blas de Otero. They are both good examples of the extreme reaction against modernism.

Celaya's early poetry borrows quite heavily from Lorca and other modernists:

Por el fondo del piano/hecho de agua en penumbra,/pasan lentos
peces blancos/entre líquenes colgantes,/entre largas algas mus-
tias/y los catorce reflejos/de catorce lunas turbias[9]
(*In the depths of the piano made of enshadowed water, pass slow
white fish between hanging lichens, between wilted seaweeds and the
fourteen images of fourteen moons ...*)

After 1950, however, a crisis of conscience turned Celaya away from
such modernist dream worlds towards an extreme anti-subjectivism
and radicalism. This led to a wholly utilitarian theory of poetry:

Recémoslo: nadie es nadie. Busquemos nuestra salvación en la
obra común, ... Salvémonos así, aquí, ahora mismo, en la acción
que nos conjunta. No seamos poetas que aúllan como perros
solitarios en la noche del crimen. ... Cantemos para todos los que
aún humillados, aún martirizados, sienten la elevadora y com-
bativa confianza propia de los plena, hermosaí, tremenda y casa
ferozmente vivos. No vayamos hacia los demás para hablarles de
nuestra peculiaridad. Abandonemos la miserable tentación de
hacer perdurable nuestro ser ensimismado. Seamos como esos
poetas—los grandes, los únicos, los universales—que en lugar de
hablarnos desde fuera, como en un confesonario, hablan en
nosotros, hablan como si fuéramos nosotros y provocan esa
identificación con ellos, o de ellos con nosotros, que certifica su
autenticidad. (p. 501)
(*Let us pray it: nobody is anybody. Let us seek our salvation in
common effort ... Let us save ourselves thus, here, now, in action
which brings us together. Let us not be poets baying like solitary
hounds on the night of the crime ... Let us sing for all those who, still
humiliated, still martyred, feel the ennobling and combative assurance
of men who are beautifully, tremendously and almost fiercely alive.
Let us not go to others to tell them about our own singularity. Let us
abandon the wretched temptation to eternalize our own self-absorbed
being. Let us be like those poets—the great, the only, universal ones—
who instead of speaking to us from without as in a confessional, speak
within us and stimulate that identification with them, or of them with
us, which guarantees their authenticity.*)

This anti-individualism led Celaya to doubt the worth of poetry
itself, and misgivings about the morality of the lyrical mode are
common enough in the social poetry movement. Since, in Celaya's

view, the function of poetry is to create consciousness among the oppressed, the poet must identify with the common people 'in order then to win over and raise that people, by means of prosaicism or whatever, until he achieves certainly NOT absolute poetry, because poetry is not an end in itself, but a state of consciousness which allows us to look back at our own works over our shoulders' (p. 46). This repudiation of poetry as a self-justifying activity leads to patent guilt about writing poetry at all:

Ya no soy poeta (¡es una ventaja!). (p. 324)
(*I'm no longer a poet. [It's an advantage!]*)
La nueva poesía sin autor que amanece/adelanta la santa conciencia de un nosotros. (p. 519)
(*The new poetry without an author which is dawning advances the sacred awareness of an Us.*)
Se hojean febrilmente los anuarios buscando/la profesión poeta—¡ay nunca registrada! (p. 503)
(*Feverishly you leaf through the directories looking for the profession poet—alas, never listed!*)
No quisiera hacer versos;
quisiera solamente contar lo que me pasa ... (p. 284)
(*I don't want to write verse; I merely want to tell what happens to me ...*)
yo cuento mis bobadas (no sé si es poesía). (p. 290)
(*I tell about the silly little things that happen to me. [I don't know if it's poetry.]*)
... escribiría un poema perfecto/si no fuera indecente hacerlo en estos tiempos. (p. 297)
(*I'd write a perfect poem, if it wasn't indecent to do that in times like these.*)

In fact Celaya thought for a time that poetry writing was quite an unremarkable activity:

Debemos comprender que el don poético no es una cosa extraordinaria, y que nadie debe tener motivo de enorgullecerse por haber hecho un buen poema. (p. 500)
(*We must grasp that the poetic gift is nothing out of the ordinary, and that no one should have grounds for pride at having written a good poem.*)

His rejection of 'pure' and *avant-garde* poetry is made in predictable terms. In 'Vivir para ver' (pp. 632–7), dedicated to 'a poet of yesterday', he denounces the 'delirious' poetry which 'used to fascinate me'; he attacks *avant-garde* writers for the feebleness of their revolutionary attitudes and their 'barely comprehensible' poetry. 'Being a poet is not enough', poetry must concern itself with the people; 'twenty years' separate Celaya from such poetry. Poets who dedicate themselves to pure poetry should remember that *'ser neutrales es pronunciarse en contra'* ('being neutral is to declare oneself against').

The verse which emerges from this programme represents a radical new departure in the history of modern Spanish poetry. Accepting from pre-War poetry the example of Antonio Machado alone, Celaya bases his poetic language almost wholly on colloquial usage and simple effects of rhyme and rhythm. But even as political verse Celaya's left-wing poetry remains unconvincing. The obstacle in the way of Celaya's programme for 'creating consciousness' and for transforming the world ('poetry is an instrument, among others, for changing the world') lies in his own outlook. Politically Celaya protests; but his instinct is to affirm that everyday life and commonplace experience are sufficient in themselves. This satisfaction with the world as he finds it works against the urge to change it; and, as for creating consciousness among the proletariat, Celaya is too anxious merely to identify with them:

> No soy muy inteligente, como se comprende,
> pero me complace saberme uno de tantos
> y en ser vulgarcillo hallo cierto descanso. (p. 287)
> Soy feliz y, por eso, también un poco tonto. (p. 289)
> Me gustan los objetos que aquí mido, aquí peso,
> y me gustan los hombres que hablan o que callan;
> me gusta cuanto existe, lo entienda o no lo entienda,
> y me gusta simplemente porque está existiendo. (p. 294)
> (*I'm not very bright as you can see,/but I like knowing I'm one of many,/and I get a sort of relief from just being ordinary . . .*
> *I'm happy, and that's why I'm a bit stupid . . .*
> *I like the objects I can measure and touch round me,/and I like people who talk or don't talk;/I like everything that exists whether I understand it or not,/and I like it simply because it is existing.*)

This urge to be like the rest leads to a certain condescendence which is far from revolutionary. One poem comments on some friends, one who reads only popular magazines and Thomas à Kempis, and the other who can only say of himself that he has caught a hundred trout:

Y esto, quizá necio,
yo lo encuentro hermoso.
¡Saben limitarse! ¡Saben ser dichosos!
Son buenos amigos que, aunque leen mis versos,/aguantan sus
ganas de escupirme encima. (pp. 325–6)
(*And although it may be silly,/I find this beautiful./They know how to
limit themselves! They know how to be happy!/They're good friends
who read my poems and still manage to fight down their urge to spit on
me.*)

A similar attitude is found in his well-known poem to Sancho Panza
as a symbol of the common people ('Sancho-good, Sancho-clay,
Sancho-people ...'). It is a danger which threatens any populist
literature written by a member of the literary elite: that of valuing the
common people *as* plebeians, of universalizing their culture as intrinsically superior. Celaya's progressive credentials are above suspicion,
but his social poetry is an example of how admiration of the *pueblo* can
lead to nostalgia for their way of life. The precedents for such populism in Spain are found not so much in progressive writers such as
Galdós, but in reactionary Catholics such as Fernán Caballero and
Pereda. These nineteenth-century conservatives were also anti-
capitalists, but their defence of the organic community of rural Spain
was backward-looking: they were reacting not against the immobility
of Spanish society, but against changes brought about by liberalism
and Europeanization. It is understandable why there should be similar feelings of nostalgia for popular life in modern Spain, but it is not
easy to see how a romantic sentimentalization of the *pueblo* has much
to do with progressive politics.

Blas de Otero

The other famous 'social' poet was Blas de Otero. Together with
Celaya he did much to establish and consolidate the anti-lyrical mode
in post-War Spanish poetry. Like Celaya, Otero abandoned his early
formal poetry after his conversion to Socialism, but in his committed
verse he tried to be more openly political than Celaya. This openness
led him into the artistic impasse which awaits any left-wing poet under
a right-wing dictatorship.

The poems 'Pido la paz y la palabra', 'En castellano', 'Ángel fieramente humano' and 'Redoble de conciencia' are based on an intense, almost religious humanism and are meant to be pro-Communist:

Apreté la voz/como un cincho, alrededor/del verso./(Salté/del horror a la fe.)/Apreté la voz./Como una mano/alrededor del mango de un martillo/de la empeñadura de una hoz.[10]
(*I drew my voice/like a girth, round/poetry. ('I leapt from horror to faith.) I clenched my voice/like a hand/round the shaft of a hammer/round the handle of a sickle.*)

The commitment is a little more explicit, for the reader who can identify the names, in 'La soledad se abre hambrientamente':

Todos los nombres que llevé en las manos/—César, Nazim, Antonio, Vladimiro,/Paul, Gabriel, Pablo, Nicolás, Miguel,/ Aragon, Rafael y Mao—, humanos/ángeles, fulgen, suenan como un tiro/único, abierto en paz sobre el papel. (p. 157)
(*Every name I bore in my hands/—César [Vallejo], Nazim [Hikmet], Antonio [Machado], Vladimiro [Lenin], Paul [Eluard], Gabriel [Celaya?], Pablo [Neruda], Nicolás [Guillén], Miguel [Hernández?], Louis [Aragon], Rafael [Alberti] and Mao—, human/angels, shining, sounding like/a unique shot, opened in peace upon the page.*)

Like Celaya, Otero also repudiated his earlier poetry (written when he was a Christian) and adopted a utilitarian poetic theory:

Ni una palabra/brotará en mis labios/que no sea verdad./Ni una sílaba/que no sea necesaria./... Destruí/los sueños, planté/ palabras/vivas. (p. 110)
(*No word/shall come from my lips/but the truth./No syllable/but is necessary./... I have destroyed/dreams, I have planted/living words.*)

Again this anti-artistic impulse leads to much guilt about poetry writing itself

... Soy sólo poeta (p. 146)
(*I'm only a poet*)
Escribo
hablando. (*Poética*, p. 123)
(*I write/talking.*)

45

Such distrust of poetic language explains the flatness of Blas de Otero's committed poetry. It also labours under other, more serious handicaps. Lacking Celaya's wry humour, much of his verse is strident moralizing. Worse than this, its message is veiled behind a smokescreen of allusions and circumlocution designed to outwit the censors. Otero constantly uses what may be described as code in order to make his political point, but the unfortunate effect is to make this poetry addressed to 'the immense majority' as cryptic as the modernist poetry he has repudiated. *MXCLV* is unintelligible to the reader without some Latin and arithmetic,

> Se ha parado el aire./En seco/el Ebro. El pulso./El Dauro/
> Oremus. El aire lleva/dieciséis años parado. (p. 127)
> (*The air has stood still./Dried up/the river Ebro. Our pulse./The river
> Dauro.* Oremus. *The air has been still/for sixteen years.*)

A favourite device of Blas de Otero is allusion to other progressive or left-wing writers or to verses from their work. Two recurrent examples are Antonio Machado and Nazim Hikmet. 'Con nosotros' (p. 101) (literally 'With Us') is a poem about Antonio Machado who 'Silent/and mysterious, joined/the people,/brandished his pen,/shook off the ash,/and went his way.' It depends for its political effect on identification of Antonio Machado as one of the author's 'human angels' alongside Mao, Lenin and others. Other poems (pp. 100 and 126) depend on allusions to poems by Machado. The full force of the lines

> Mi fe es más firme que la torre Eiffel./Vientos del pueblo/
> esculpieron su mágica estatura. (p. 106)
> (*My faith is firmer than the Eiffel Tower./Winds of the people/
> sculpted its magic stature.*)

can only be felt if we are sensitive to the allusion to Miguel Hernández's Communist book *Viento del pueblo* described previously. Such use of code and allusion ensures that Blas de Otero's message will only be clear to readers familiar with left-wing traditions and possessing a reasonable literary culture. Consequently his committed poetry rests on the elitist assumptions which the author claimed to have repudiated. This smoke-screen of allusion is imposed by the social poets' decision to publish within the state controlled book distribution system, but it involves sacrifice of the imaginative power of modernism with no real gain in intelligibility. Otero was himself aware of the way his poetic language was falsified—

hablaría yo claro, tejería
las letras de otro modo màs simplemente, si ... (p. 134)
(*I would speak clearer, weave*
letters in another simpler way, if ...)

The Collapse of Left-wing Realist Poetry

The 'social poetry' movement seems to have discredited the lyrical impulse itself—at least temporarily. If, as is often said, post-Civil War Spain was not a good environment for writing poetry, the reason lies in the vogue for this kind of politicized anti-poetry. The social poetry movement collapsed in about 1965 in one of those sudden collective repudiations and changes of direction which periodically affect the cliquish and fashion-obsessed writers of modern Spain. But one extreme begets another: the new poets of the late 1960s seem to have gone to the opposite extremes of opaque complexity. The remarks of one repentant social poet, Manuel Vázquez Montalbán, indicate the kind of crisis which overtook social poetry:

> En mis primeros versos pedía libertad, pan, justicia, enseñanza gratuita y amor libre (yo en mi adolescencia era muy tigre de papel y muy reformista).
> Ahora escribo como si fuera idiota, única actividad lúcida que puede consentirse un intelectual sometido a una organización de la cultura precariamente neocapitalista. ... Creo que la poesía, tal como está organizada la cultura, no sirve para nada. Sospecho que no sirve para nada en ninguna parte.[11]
> (*In my early verse I asked for freedom, bread, justice, free education and free love (in my youth I was a real paper tiger and reformist).*
> *Now I write as if I were an idiot, the only lucid activity an intellectual can allow himself when subjected to a precariously neocapitalist cultural system. ... I think poetry, as culture is organized at present, has no use. I suspect it never does have any use anywhere.*)

The social poetry movement collapsed because it was based on the fallacious idea that verse distributed in editions of a few hundred would directly affect the political situation of the day. While this hope was alive, poets scorned excessive artistic self-consciousness and deliberately avoided any kind of diction which was obviously poetic. Unfortunately, the inevitable disillusion which set in when the Franco regime was discovered to be almost invulnerable to criticism seems to have led to poetry based on a feckless subjectivism. It may be that these violent oscillations between populist and minority poetry will only stabilize when the potential readership inside Spain enlarges to the point where different kinds of poetry can coexist peacefully, all assured of at least some support from a numerous and critically divided—and therefore pluralistic—readership.

Chapter Four

Commitment and the Modernist Novel

The only Spanish genre to produce great works in the nineteenth century was the realist novel. The *Novelas contemporáneas* of Benito Pérez Galdós and Leopoldo Alas's monumental study of provincial life, *La Regenta* (1884), are major though neglected contributions to European realism. These novels are not politically committed. Galdós's greatest novels are a product of uncertainty in the author's mind about politics and the perfectibility of human nature. This uncertainty allows him to see most sides of an argument, and his novels get their complexity from this plural vision. Alas's *La Regenta* is likewise a product of uncertainty about, among other things, the consequences of the *embourgeoisement* of Church and moral life in the late nineteenth century. In both cases, the novels' profundity is a product of ambiguities rather than of political or moral single-mindedness.

The modernist novel is extremely heterogeneous. Some writers, like Miguel de Unamuno, came to the extreme conclusion that realism is nothing but a passive reflection of external reality incapable of saying anything about the 'real' experience of the individual. He could say this because he thought that no social or historical experience was important compared with the problem of immortality. As a result, his novels present disembodied characters set either in an indeterminate social context (e.g. *Niebla*, *Abel Sánchez*, *La tía Tula*) or in a romanticized version of Spain whose patent unreality strips the novel's message of all real credibility, as least as a comment on Spanish society if not on the human condition (e.g. *San Manuel Bueno, mártir*).

Other modernist writers also wrote de-socialized novels, or novels in which the social content is so refracted through a series of artistic devices that it is tempting to conclude that the texts are self-delighting formal exercises. Examples of these extremes of modernist anti-realism are some of the novels of Azorín, Francisco Ayala's earliest stories,[1] and some texts by Ramón Gómez de la Serna and Benjamín Jarnés.

A few struck exactly the right balance between realism and modernism. After a long private debate about the limits of aestheticism, conducted over many short stories and novels, Gabriel Miró produced the masterpieces *Nuestro padre San Daniel* (1921) and *El obispo leproso* (1926), which are penetrating analyses of nineteenth-century rural life, but move beyond any limited realism thanks to a complex symbolic structure. Nevertheless, the social content of Miró's novels was doggedly ignored by Spanish Marxist critics of the 1950s and 1960s who failed to see beyond the 'aesthetic' surface structure to the progressive message of the novel.

Pío Baroja and the Survival of Realism

Of the major novelists of the pre-Civil War period, Pío Baroja stands out as having rejected modernism, and his example had a profound influence on later political realism. In his earliest essays he repudiated the incipient modernist movement. He detested the dandyism and self-conscious decadence of the early symbolists and aesthetes (*modernistas*); he ridiculed the '*snob simbolista*';[2] and in the magazine *La Vida Literaria* (15th May, 1899), he made an all-out attack on the anti-realist and subjective tendencies of modern literature, which, he says, work only on the subconscious and 'consist in the free exercise of cerebral automatism' which, if it affects us, 'produces a contemplative state in which the reader neither understands nor thinks reflectively'.

Baroja ascribes this irrationalism to humanity's loss of a sense of 'beauty, love and life' brought about by the triumph of his *bête noire*, Christianity. Nevertheless, his novels are not in practice like those of the realists, among whom he especially admired Dickens. They are, it is true, matter-of-fact accounts of everyday life, and their lasting value is that they give us a graphic and convincing picture of Spanish society in the early twentieth century—indeed, they provide *the* most convincing and moving account of the class conflict and injustice of the social system of the period. But they depart from nineteenth-century realism to the extent that they offer us not a 'factual' account of a situation, but a series of subjective impressions in the invariably jaundiced mind of the protagonist. We are not always invited to accept the objectivity of these impressions. In many of his novels, e.g. *El árbol de la ciencia* (1912) or *César o nada* (1910), the author dissociates himself from the protagonist, and we are invited to consider the foolishness of the latter's political and moral ideas. The result is an openness and a plurality of points of view which to some extent compensates for the relentless listlessness of his prose.

The meandering prosaicism of Baroja's novels is a far cry from the highly wrought language and structures of the modernist novelists. Baroja rejected any artistic 'elaboration' which distances the text from the world it seeks to reproduce, and the result is novels which offer a laconic, flat, unselective account of life. They can be quite astonishingly unstructured: chapters can be devoted to casual and aimless conversations with chance acquaintances which have no obvious bearing on the whole work. Politically, Baroja was no enthusiast for any particular party. His novels may be a moving account of real social problems, but he had little time for any one who tried to put them right. He held the progressive tradition in contempt, considered democracy a 'farce'; valued liberalism only for its 'destructive' potential, and seems to have staked his slight political enthusiasms only on vague hope for an enlightened dictatorship. His anti-Semitism and contempt for Socialists earned him the admiration of some Fascists, but his political isolation is best symbolized by the spur-of-the-moment decision by some Carlist militiamen to shoot him in 1936. They changed their minds to the disgust of some left-wing papers in Republican Madrid.[3]

Valle-Inclán: A Solution to the Problem of Committed anti-Realism

Despite these dubious political credentials, Baroja's novels were much admired by post-War critics and authors of the social realist movement. It was his novels rather than the modernists' which became a model for post-War anti-Franco realism; a choice full of consequences for the form of that literature. It was an ironic and unfortunate choice, because a brilliant alternative model for the political novel existed. Ramón del Valle-Inclán's fiction and plays offer a unique solution to the vexed question of the relationship between progressive political commitment and realist techniques. Single-handed he advanced to a position not dissimilar to Brecht's—of whom, to my knowledge, he had never heard. Had post-Civil War novelists not been blinded to his work by anti-modernist prejudice, they might have produced a brilliant and original series of Socialist novels.

Valle's political writings, *Tirano banderas* (1926), a study of a Latin

American dictator, the *El ruedo ibérico* series (1927–32) on the Liberal revolution of 1868, and the plays *Luces de bohemia* (1920), the *Martes de carnaval* trilogy (1930) and others, are neglected satirical masterpieces which contain a lesson for any committed writer. Valle's development as a political writer is rather odd. He began in the most aloof and elitist literary movement imaginable—as an imitator of *décadents* such as Barbey d'Aurevilly and the early D'Annunzio. From these he took a literary language and an aristocratic *persona* which provided him with an artistic standpoint quite unlike that of the nineteenth-century realists. Initially he was (or affected to be) committed to extreme reactionary Carlism, and a brilliant but caricatural aping of the *hidalgo* manner typified both his work and life. But his treatment of Carlist themes was deliberately sentimental and parodic: the exquisite stylization of the works constantly reminds us that we have to do with a literary artefact, not with an image of real life: Valle was too intelligent to take Carlist politics seriously. At about the same time he was dabbling in occultism, and although it is difficult to judge the seriousness of this interest (as with most of his attitudes), it is clear that gnostic transcendentalism provided him with yet another mythical basis for a refusal of realism in literature. Valle exploited gnosticism to increase the distance between his work and reality. In his occultist treatise on literature, *La lámpara maravillosa* (1916), he advocated emotional aloofness from reality: 'for the ecstatic there is no change in the images of the world, for he knows how to love them with equal love in all their aspects, mindful of the eternal act by which they are created . . .'[4] *La lámpara maravillosa* argues that the artist should detach himself from direct emotional involvement in his subject matter and redirect his attention to techniques—especially to renewing worn-out language—which will help him to produce an aesthetically perfect text.

Had Valle stopped here, his work might have been simply one more brilliant addition to a long line of *fin-de-siècle* rejections of modern life for the swans and lilies of aestheticism. But Valle's originality lies in the fact that having thus equipped himself with an aesthetic which stresses distance between art and reality he began, after the First World War, to write almost exclusively about politics. After 1920 the subjects of his work became militarism, revolution, governmental corruption, police brutality, class struggle and the endless follies of the Spanish Bourbon regime.

This unusual transition by no means involved a repudiation of his earlier techniques. In a brief essay on a visit to the trenches of northern France, Valle stated that his intention was to offer an 'astral' vision of the war, 'outside the geometry of time'. He therefore wrote of the horrors of the trenches in a quaint, mannered prose which superficially reflects an almost total lack of emotional response. The tension, however, between form and content is deliberately shocking—and it is this contrast between a deliberately highly wrought and dispassionate form and tragic content that is central to the *'esperpento'* technique as Valle called it. (The word means, roughly, 'grotesque sight' or 'ludicrous apparition'.)

Valle frequently insists on the need for art to deform reality. One of his characters compares the technique with those distorting mirrors which throw back a ludicrous version of the original: such grotesque images, he claims, are the only ones which can do justice to 'the tragic sense of Spanish life' (*Luces de Bohemia*, scene 12). This recalls Brecht's dissatisfaction with the way ordinary realism produces a numbing empathy in the reader or audience. The *esperpento* technique uses all kinds of alienation devices—puppetry, archaic, invented or sub-standard vocabulary, stylized gestures, the rhetoric of cheap journalism—in order to put the audience at a distance from the events portrayed. Events which are in themselves shocking examples of poverty, violence and exploitation are treated as though their main significance were aesthetic. Perhaps the most remarkable aspect of Valle's work is the creation of a literary language which refuses to be imprisoned by linguistic register. It moves constantly from street slang to the refined lexicon of the *symboliste*, from cheap romance to Baroque eloquence, from rural dialect to journalese, within the same passage. The effect is to produce a bizarre dialect which no reader or audience member will easily identify as his own. He will be *forced* to listen. I understand this as a perfect application of the principles of Brecht. Unfortunately it would take a Joyce to translate Valle into English.

Socialist Realism under Franco

Despite Valle's excellent solution to the problem of how to write political literature which uses formal experiments to dramatize the political message, post-Civil War social and political realists ignored his example and imitated the lacklustre prose of Pío Baroja and similar

53

writers. This is true both of non-political protest novels such as Cela's *La familia de Pascual Duarte* (1942), Carmen Laforet's *Nada* (1945), and Fernández Santos's *Los bravos* (1954), and of the committed left-wing realist novels of the *novela social* movement to be described below. Rediscovery of Valle-Inclán's political work was, as a result, delayed for several decades after 1939—until, in fact, the premises of social realism were questioned in the mid-1960s.

As with the poetry, the collapse of the modernist novel in Spain can in part be explained by historical circumstances. Valle-Inclán and Gabriel Miró both died before the Civil War, and Unamuno shortly after its outbreak; Francisco Ayala and Benjamín Jarnés went into exile; Pérez de Ayala wrote no more novels. Only Baroja and 'Azorín' continued to write inside Spain, the former an ageing solitary and the latter too hopelessly compromised with the conservative right to inspire younger writers. Other circumstances, however, explain the disappearance of the modernist prose tradition. On top of the political distrust of modernism described in previous chapters, the special circumstances of the Franco regime imposed a peculiar function on social realism in the period from 1939 to 1965. Literature attracted less attention from the authorities than the mass media, including the theatre. As a result there is no doubt that the realist novel usurped some of the functions of the press in a free society: that of disseminating facts about everyday life in Spain to readers who could get no information from other sources. Coupled with the repudiation of modernism, this meant the triumph in Spain of a crude reflective realism as the predominant narrative mode among opposition writers until the 1960s. This in itself explains the uninspiring quality of many post-Civil War realist novels in that period. Add to it the crushing pessimism which fills the novels of Cela and Laforet and also many socialist realist works—a pessimism consecrated as a new literary 'ism', *tremendismo*, the exaggerated description of pain, degradation, perversion, misfortune and sordidness—and the result is one of the gloomiest, bitterest series of novels in European literature.

A *novela social* movement emerged in the 1950s, the prose counterpart of the politicized *poesía social* school of the same period.[5] It would in normal circumstances have been called the *novela socialista* movement, had it been possible publicly to identify one's real politics in those years. The special meaning in Franco's Spain of the word 'social' is revealed in such tactfully discreet definitions of the *novela social* as 'that which tries to show the rigidity of a society, or the inequality or injustice at its heart'.[6] The vindictive Alfonso Sastre jibes at the 'social' writers as 'left-wing opportunists' who promoted 'a highly anti-Franco literature'.[7] Some of the 'social' authors have since openly spoken of their previous political enthusiasms: one, Armando López Salinas, is today an official spokesman of the Communist Party of Spain.

The movement is associated with novelists such as Antonio Ferres, Armando López Salinas, Jesús López Pacheco, Juan Goytisolo, Juan García Hortelano, Juan Marsé and others. The group was actively supported by the well-known publisher Carlos Barral, and its critical *doyen* was José María Castellet who provided the most important Spanish theoretical defence of the special link between left-wing politics and realist techniques.

Castellet's theoretical work is an excellent example of an application of Machado's belief that a truly humanist literature would require the replacement of subjective idealism by 'objectivism'. Castellet argued that a dispassionate mirroring of reality is a precondition of progressive literature. Any attempt to distance the text from the reality it describes is condemned as symptomatic of the subjection of literature to bourgeois ideology. This argument is put forward most cogently in his *La hora del lector* (Barcelona, 1957), a work widely discussed by left-wing intellectuals of the day. Castellet links the constant presence of the author in the texts of nineteenth-century realism with the triumphant self-confidence of the bourgeoisie of the day. The development of stream-of-consciousness techniques signified the 'loss of bourgeois security and social order', since authors were now openly admitting that their point of view was purely subjective and relative. The gradual self-effacement of the author as an active presence in the text is thus evidence, in Castellet's view, of the way modern authors are dissociating themselves from bourgeois ideology and adopting a progressive position. Twentieth-century literature, under the 'objectivizing' influence of the cinema, is relying increasingly on the presentation of images without comment as writers commit themselves more and more to mere description of 'human behaviour in situation':

> En efecto, al limitarse el autor a narrar objetivamente o por así decirlo, *desde fuera*, situaciones dadas, se niega a sí mismo toda posibilidad de analizar, juzgar, recomponer o comentar la conducta de sus personajes, como gustaba de hacer el autor

decimonónico. Con ello el novelista da testimonio de—y se compromete con—el pensamiento más avanzado de su tiempo. (pp. 37–8)

Las técnicas nuevas, en especial la de las *narraciones objetivas*, han rescatado [al autor] de su pedestal decimonónico y le han devuelto, junto con su condición de hombre, su dignidad humana . . . Todo ello ha hecho posible que la novela de nuestro siglo tenga como cualidad fundamental su inquietud por todos los problemas humanos vistos a través de una pluralidad de enfoques narrativos, y, especialmente, de un tono general de objetividad, básicos para un posible entendimiento y mutua colaboración entre autor y lector. Situados en un mismo plano, ambos se encuentran ante la novela con las mismas posibilidades de liberación. (pp. 40–1)

(Indeed, by limiting himself to an objective account of given situations from outside, so to speak, the author denies himself any possibility of analysing, judging, retouching or commenting on the conduct of his characters—which was the sort of thing the nineteenth-century writer liked to do. By doing this the novelist bears witness to—and commits himself to—the most advanced thought of his day . . . The new techniques, especially the technique of objective narrative, have rescued the author from his nineteenth-century pedestal and have returned to him both his status as a man and his human dignity . . . The effect of this has been that the novel of our century is essentially characterized by its concern for all human problems approached from a multiplicity of narrative viewpoints, and above all by an overall tone of objectivity—essential for eventual understanding and mutual collaboration between author and reader. Finding themselves on the same plane, both discover, faced with the novel, the same possibilities of freedom.)

'*Behaviorismo*' or objective narrative is a feature which distinguishes post-Civil War Spanish realism from that of the nineteenth century. It is difficult to see how the conflicting ideals of an 'author-less', objective narrative and left-wing commitment can be reconciled in the same text. The answer, in the practice of Socialist novels, is of course a ruthless selection of the worst features of Spanish society which are then presented by the author without comment. But Castellet avoids concessions to moral authoritarianism by suggesting that the mere presentation of reality in an objective way is itself a progressive act. On these grounds he welcomed Sánchez Ferlosio's novel *El Jarama* (1956)—an insipid and meandering account of a day in the life of a group of youths—as a 'moral' work which would renew our contact with 'reality' and help us to escape from subjective idealism.[8] The argument is the same as Machado's about the moral as well as literary imperative of a new objectivism for social renewal.

Juan Goytisolo argued along similar lines. In *Problemas de la novela* (1959) he also defended *behaviorismo* as an overdue acknowledgment of the reader's critical freedom. He admired the 'neutrality' of Baroja in comparison with Unamuno's moralizing (p. 11), but made the defence of objectivism more overtly political than did Castellet. The psychological novel, which objectivism was now to supersede, presupposes articulate characters capable of the intricacies of thought and feeling which the form demanded. These were inevitably sophisticated and therefore bourgeois characters: 'the near totality of novels published in Spain in the last thirty years is concerned with a select minority—the middle and upper classes' (p. 18). For this reason, Cela's *La colmena*, Santos' *Los bravos*, and *El Jarama* are first steps towards a novel of the proletariat and peasantry. Goytisolo thus extended the behaviourist argument by implying that objectivism is peculiarly suited for the depiction of working-class life. The inversion of sane critical values to which this 'behaviourist' realism can lead is well demonstrated in one of his conclusions:

> Mientras que las novelas de Galdós y Baroja dan una imagen fiel de la sociedad española de su tiempo, las novelas de Miró, Unamuno y Pérez de Ayala no reflejan absolutamente nada. (p. 84)
>
> (*Whereas Galdós's and Baroja's novels give a faithful image of the Spanish society of their day, the novels of Miró, Unamuno and Pérez de Ayala reflect absolutely nothing.*)

Both Goytisolo's and Castellet's arguments are applications of Ortega's assumption that realism is the art form of a particular social class or of democratic or populist ideology. But there is nothing particularly progressive about the ideology underlying Cela's *La colmena* (1951), *El Jarama* or Baroja's novels. Cela's novel voices an uncompromising nihilism: 'I would like to develop the idea that a healthy man has no ideas'. *El Jarama* is part of the Barojan tradition of using images of social degradation as symbols of the general absurdity of the human condition. Goytisolo says in *Problemas de la novela* that the meaning of this novel lies in its technique. But the technique is, inevitably, a comment on the proletarian characters of the novel; on their hopes and their human potential. The aimless structure, the flat, unemotive language, the atmosphere of banality and torpor, the overwhelming presence of the sluggish and unchanging river, invite a conclusion which also bears on the future of the world depicted by the novel. A typical passage, near the end, summarizes the events of the book:

> Lucio saltó al camino y orinó interminablemente, a la luz de la luna, que ya casi tocaba el horizonte sobre las lomas de Coslada. A sus espaldas oía cerrarse la puerta de Mauricio, y cuando echó a andar de nuevo, ya había desaparecido el rectángulo de luz que salía de la venta. La carretera le llevaba entre dos olivares hasta las mismas tapias de San Fernando, y el ruido del agua del río sonando allá abajo en la compuerta se dejaba de oír súbitamente, al quedar interceptado por detrás de los primeros edificios. Eran casitas muy nuevas, de ladrillo a la vista, y aún la mayoría sin habitar.[9]
>
> (*Lucio jumped out onto the road and urinated interminably, in the light of the moon now almost touching the horizon on the hills of Coslada. Behind him he heard Mauricio's door shutting, and when he began walking again the rectangle of light from the inn had already vanished. The road took him between two olive groves right up to the walls of San Fernando, and the sound of river water from floodgates far below suddenly ceased as it was cut off behind the first buildings. They were small, very new houses of bare brick, most of them still untenanted.*)

Such a passage is saturated with ideological subjectivism. It forms the conclusion of the novel and is followed by a descriptive passage of the Jarama flowing finally to the sea. The urine, declining moon, disappearing light and quietening water are symbolic of the futility which the novel describes. The vision of *El Jarama* is that of the apolitical scepticism of Baroja, Cela, and of Carmen Laforet's *Nada*.

Cela and Sánchez Ferlosio, however, established a style which social realism appropriated. In practice, 'objectivism' in the *novela social* meant not the systematic application of Goytisolo's and Castellet's theories about the disappearance of the author, but the adoption of a laconic, spiritless descriptive technique to be found everywhere in the Spanish realist novel between about 1955 and 1963. The following passages are characteristic of the effects of this reduction of realism to 'objectivism'.

> Gregorio detuvo el automóvil y preguntó por cuarta vez. El hombre extendió el brazo.
> Siga hasta el poste. Allí, tuerza por el camino, a la derecha. No tiene pérdida.
> La senda carecía de comunicación con la carretera. El Automóvil osciló al pasar la cuneta. La extensión de los campos, solitarios y pardos, desconcertó a Gregorio. No aparecía edificación alguna por los alrededores. Continuó, avanzando lentamente por el estrecho camino; tras él, quedaba una trasparente masa de polvo blanquísimo. El camino se inclinó en una pendiente, después de la curva. Gregorio frenó. Aquello era el poblado, la chata superficie de manchas que, unos minutos antes desde la carretera, había supuesto hornos de cal o ruinas. Mas allá del alcance de sus ojos, permanecían las chabolas. Acabó la cuesta y en una extensión libre del terreno, Gregorio maniobró hasta dejar el coche con el morro orientado hacia la senda. Aseguró el cierre de las ventanillas y las portezuelas.[10]
> (Gregorio stopped the car and asked a fourth time. The man stretched out his arm. "Go as far as the post. Then turn right. You can't miss it." The path did not run out into the road. The car jolted as it went over the verge. The expanse of fields, solitary and brown, disconcerted Gregorio. There was no building anywhere around. He went on slowly up the narrow track; behind him hung a bright mass of white dust. The track went downhill after the curve. Gregorio braked. It was the hamlet, the squat set of blurred marks which a moment before on the road, he had taken for lime kilns or ruins. Further beyond, out of sight, were the shacks. The slope ended and on a free stretch of ground he turned to leave his car facing the track. He checked the windows and the doors were shut.)

El señor Remigio se encontraba como sobre ascuas. Deseaba que regresara pronto su vecino. Quería saber si había sacado algo en claro con el aparejador. Desde que estuvo en casa de Andrés se encontraba lleno de inquietud. El viejo tenía alquilado una habitación, que daba al corral, en una chabola de al lado, en otra de las casuchas que formaban aquella especie de calle sobre la loma, delante del cerro.

No paraba de salir a la puerta, por ver si regresaba Andrés. Era

ya noche cerrada. Se oían, mezclados con el silencio, todos los
rumores que surgían del campo. Del cielo venía mucho fulgor.
No había luna, pero brillaban las estrellas y el Camino de San-
tiago parecía más ancho y luminoso que nunca.[11]
*(Señor Remigio was on tenterhooks. He wanted his neighbour to come
back soon. He wanted to know if he had got anywhere with the
foreman. Ever since he had been at Andrés's place he had been full of
anxieties. The old man had rented a room, looking out on the yard, in
the next-door shack, in one of the other little huts which formed a sort
of street on the rise leading up to the ridge.*
*He went constantly to the door to see if Andrés was returning. It was
already quite dark. Mingled with the silence were all the noises from
the fields. The sky was bright. There was no moon, but the stars were
shining, and the Milky Way seemed brighter and wider than ever.)*

Juan Goytisolo and Armando López Salinas

'Objectivism', which is a natural development from a prose style
innovated by Baroja and developed by Cela and Sánchez Ferlosio, is a
language of despair. It suggests an unbridgeable gap between the
author and an alienated world, and this is nowhere more evident than
in the 'objective' writers' treatment of characters. The technique is
based on a refusal to speculate about a character's psychology. But a
technique which rejects all departures from strict empiricism would
also exclude the possibility of suggesting that beneath a monotonous
exterior, there might lie a wealth of half- or unrealized life, un-
expressed because of environment. To this extent the *behaviorista*
method gives the impression, deliberate or not, that the writer is
describing persons or groups to which he is a total outsider, which he
does not understand and from which he expects nothing. The objectivist manner, where it affects the *novela social*, works against what
ought to be the idealistic and revolutionary content of these novels.

These remarks can, I believe, be applied to a greater or lesser extent
to the socialist realist works of García Hortelano, Antonio Ferres,
López Pacheco and others. None of them systematically applied
objectivist theory, but all write in a prose style which suffers from the
lack of vitality which comes from deliberately eschewing any kind of
writing which departs from a purely mechanical recording of observed
facts.

Few works can be said to have survived from the *novela social* movement. Those that have seem to bear out the conclusions I have suggested, that the objectivist technique makes an ideal of mediocrity. The most famous novels of the periods, the political novels of Juan Goytisolo (who, ironically was a theoretical advocate of objectivism) and López Salinas, escaped the effects of behaviourism and retained many of the 'subjective' features deplored by the objectivist critics.

It is doubtful, however, whether Goytisolo's political novels can be said to be committed. *El circo* (1957), *La resaca* (1958), *La Isla* (1961), *La chanca* (1962), *Fin de fiesta* (1962) argue little more than a generalized pessimism about Spain. They are all a prelude to his anti-realist novel *La reivindicación del conde don Julián* (1970), a sophisticated diatribe against all things Spanish—'Land of three-cornered hats and a people which puts up with them—I shall never return to you'.

La resaca is a good example. Its theme is the hopelessness of Spanish politics and the intractability of the Spanish temperament in the face of progressive ideals.

It depicts two groups. Antonio's group, one suspects, represents Goytisolo's real assessment of the possibilities of Spanish society: a gang of street urchins exploits a Church charity-drive with the help of the innocent Antonio, whose rake's progress into crime, perversion and disillusion is described in sensational detail. He is seduced in a goods wagon by a young prostitute and abandoned by his fellow thieves.

Against this *lumpenproletariat* background, the two idealists, Giner and Emilio, labour to organize a working-class movement. Their hopes collapse because Goytisolo's working class really consists of little more than grotesque *pícaros*. In the middle of a clandestine meeting of militants which is discussing methods of organizing a strike among the doctors, 'Cinco Duros' and 'Cien Gramos' break in drunk, singing Socialist songs, and turn the meeting into a farce. The novel ends in arrests, disillusion and suicide, but Goytisolo appends a colophon from Machado, 'But another Spain is being born,/a Spain of the chisel and the mallet'. Nothing in the novel invites this belief of Machado's in the future. The quotation is added, as it were, to supply that commitment to radical politics which the novel does not really contain.

The masterpiece of the *novela social* movement is Armando López Salinas' *Año tras año* (Paris, 1962), a novel which has fallen into scandalous neglect. Written by a member of the Communist Party, it

61

succeeds as committed realism because it avoids both the insipid prose of objectivism and political despair. It depicts the lives of a large number of Madrid working-class characters in the years 1939 to 1955, a period when the fortunes of the Spanish working-class movement were at their lowest. A Socialist account of a defeated working class might well invite the despair of Cela, Laforet or Goytisolo, but López Salinas' theme is the irrepressible spirit of the proletariat. Nor does the author's optimism lapse into crude romanticizing about the workers. He portrays the proletariat convincingly by balancing the negative and positive features of his characters in such a way as to do justice to the real problems of Socialist organization.

López Salinas realizes that, when times are bad, the spirit of rebellion takes refuge in sullen non-cooperation and humour. His characters set about subverting the 'New Order' within days of the Nationalists' triumphant entry into Madrid. First they find ways round the need for *avales* or certificates of political reliability; once inside the factories they put pressure on the management for better conditions; by the end of the novel the younger generation has organized successful strikes and a boycott of public transport. Enrique is arrested and tortured by the Spanish police for illegal propaganda, but by now enough members of the group are sufficiently politicized to keep up the fight. The novel ends thus:

—Está muy sucio todo—dijo Joaquín como avergonzado.
—No te preocupes, se arreglará.
—A mí no me gusta esta casa, tiene algo que no me gusta. Quizá me recuerde cosas poco agradables. Yo la dejaría contento, la dejaría igual que se abandona una vieja idea o una antigua creencia—dijo Juan.
—Es la única que tenemos. Esta casa es como España, sucia y fea. Pero se puede arreglar. Habrá que cambiarlo todo, habrá que hundir la piqueta hasta que salga el rojo de los ladrillos.
Joaquín quedó en silencio escuchando a la muchacha. Luego, también ésta calló. A través de la ventana abierta, desde abajo, de la calle, llegaba el ruido de la vida. (p. 312)
(*"All of this is pretty dirty," Joaquin said, as if ashamed.*
"Don't worry, we'll put it right."
"I don't like this house, there's something about it I don't like. Perhaps it reminds me of unpleasant things. I'd leave it happily, the same as you give up an old idea or belief," Juan said.

"It's the only one we've got. This house is like Spain, dirty and ugly. But it can be put right. It'll have to be changed from top to bottom, you'll have to put the pick in until the red spurts out of the bricks." Joaquin fell silent listening to the girl. Then she too fell silent. Through the open window, from below, in the street, came the sound of life.)

In the context of the novel this is an effective ending. López Salinas's working class includes *beatas* (pious old women), Fascists, cynics or 'characters' who are simply confused, such as Don José, a 'Socialist' who admires 'Rusvelt' (*'los tiene bien puestos'*) and Mussolini—although 'that fool with the Charlie Chaplin moustache called Hitler has gone to his head'.

The novel's dialogues are unforgettable. The author's knowledge of working-class slang is tremendous and he understands how (usually obscene) humour keeps a sense of solidarity alive. Hunted by vindictive Fascists, out of work and starving, the characters can still joke endlessly about pretty girls. A single remark can suddenly make decades of Fascist indoctrination seem ridiculous. Joaquín is doing military service and chatting with his fellow soldiers:

La botella pasó de boca en boca.
—Ayer estuve en San Marcos pisándome a la Remi.
—La Remi hace el 'francés'. Te saca los tuétanos en cuanto te descuidas.
—Como te oiga el capellán se te va a caer el pelo.
—Entonces¿pa qué nos dan la bolsita con el profilático?¿Pa ir a la doctrina?
(The bottle circulated from mouth to mouth.
'I was in San Marcos yesterday screwing "la Remi".'
'"La Remi" does it the French way. She'll have your joints out if you don't watch it.'
'If the chaplain hears you, you won't half cop it.'
'Then what do they give us the little bag with the rubber in for? To go to catechism classes?'

In *La mina*, (1960) López Salinas makes a similar point. The novel tells of an Andalusian peasant who moves north to seek a better life in the coal mines. After much heroic suffering he is killed in an accident caused not by fate or bad luck, but by the management's neglect of safety precautions. Yet, as in the previous novel, the author does not question human nature: the characters retain their humour and

63

patience throughout, and the widow can balance her loss against her love for her children. Both novels end on a hopeful note: the society they present is not congenitally or racially corrupt, but the victim of a specific regime which can be altered.

To ask for historical optimism from left-wing writers in Franco's Spain is to expect much. The pressures on opposition writers to portray their society in the blackest possible terms must have been very great. Indeed, there is a sense in which such pessimism is itself politically subversive. The state-controlled media presented Spain as a Christian and morally uncontaminated country little affected by the permissiveness of western democracies. To fill novels with reports of prostitution, perversion, sadism, addiction and abortions therefore challenged the official version of Spanish history as a long-delayed affirmation of Catholic virtues. Thus *tremendismo* can be understood as a political attack on official mythology: the tragic sense of life becomes subversive in situations where official ideology is optimistic. Not for nothing does official Soviet criticism condemn pessimistic books.

But radical commitment requires historical optimism, and the *novela social*, with the exceptions mentioned, does not supply it. If novels portray the Nationalist victory of 1939 as the irremediable end of progressive hopes in Spain and as the effective conclusion of the class struggle, then whatever their artistic qualities they remain examples of the type of protest realism found in Baroja, Cela and Laforet: the presentation of political crisis as symbolic of a tragic human condition.

Such literature need not be written in language accessible to the working classes, for they are beyond hope; and it seems to me that it was the realization of this fact which generated the reaction against the *novela social* inaugurated by Martín Santos's *Tiempo de silencio* (1962) and carried forward in the later works of Juan Goytisolo (*Señas de identidad*, *La reivindicación del Conde don Julián*, *Juan sin tierra*) and in those of Luis Goytisolo (*Recuento*, *Los verdes de mayo hasta el mar*), José-María Guelbenzu and Juan Benet.[12] Structurally these novels involve a return to the complexities of modernism—carried to extremes in the cases of the Goytisolo brothers and Juan Benet. But they contain the same pessimism as the *novela social*—the same accounts of drunkenness, promiscuity and perversion which undermined the progressive vision of the Socialist novels. To this extent the 'new' Spanish novel of the 1970s involves not a deeply changed attitude towards Spanish society, which all agree was a hopeless case until Franco's death, but a logical application of the view that literature cannot really affect the situation. The almost unreadable complexity of some recent Spanish novels amounts to a confession that 'art' is useless. Social realism can only really survive and produce fine works when authors believe with Armando López Salinas, that their society is truly worth writing about.

Conclusion

The history of Spanish literature has been characterized by a polarization between potentially popular literature and literature which could never be popular. The country has produced vivid works which go deep into the life of the common people for their themes and language—the medieval ballads, the epic of the Cid, Lope de Vega's plays, *Lazarillo de Tormes* and *Don Quixote* itself. On the other hand it has also produced works of such refinement, complexity or otherworldliness that all reference to the common life seems to have been distilled out of them. Góngora is, of course, the classic example: 'I am more than honoured to be obscure to the ignorant . . . precious stones are not thrown to swine'.

This polarization has given rise to debate in the past about the merits of the two kinds of literature, but it was not until modern times that it became politicized. With Ortega's judgment that realism is the technique of mass art, the traditional argument about popular and minority literature was absorbed into the general battle between progress and reaction. Given the savage polarization of Spanish life it is not surprising that the controversy should have been pushed to extremes. In the last twenty years the poles have been the *novela social* and the 'new' novel of the 1970s. In the 1930s they were, for example, the impenetrable verse of Emilio Prados and the prose of Pío Baroja. Occasionally the pendulum in these oscillations has paused at a midpoint between private obscurity and public banality, and produced works of great subtlety, profundity and clarity. Some have been mentioned in the preceding pages.

The absence of a large readership no doubt accounts for much of this division between populists and elitists. Spanish writers have been traditionally faced with a stark alternative: either the 'oral' tradition or court literature; either a large semi-literate or philistine audience or a thinly scattered, cosmopolitan elite. The readership for a compromise type of literature has often not existed. As a result, works addressed to the elite have tended to degenerate into a self-delighting formalism, into the sort of gratuitous verbal cleverness which is never far from the surface of much twentieth-century Spanish modernism: who but a modern Spanish poet (Miguel Hernández) could have called bullfight posters on a wall 'contemporary ivy' (*hiedra contemporánea*)? In its populist phases, on the other hand, Spanish literature has sometimes been threatened, at least in the last three hundred years, by extremes of artistic self-denial such as we find in some eighteenth-century writers, and in Núñez de Arce, Campoamor, Unamuno's and Machado's poetry, Luis Cernuda and, of course, in Otero and the social poets.

No doubt this uneasy relationship between 'art' and 'communication' operates in all European literature, although it seems that in those countries where writers can count on (or believe they can count on) a large, educated readership, a productive interaction between form and content can be established. In such circumstances texts are created out of a debate between a large, sensitive, nonspecialist readership and exacting individual artists. This could not happen in Spain. In the modern period the absence of any original literary criticism symbolizes the lack of a demanding readership. Public response in the form of articulate criticism in Spain is of low quality. It is fruitless to ask where are the Spanish Arnolds, Leavises, Richardses, Trillings, Barthes, Williamses and Northrop Fryes (with apologies for the arbitrary selection). One looks in vain to a prestigious periodical such as *Ínsula* for vigorous critical articles. A good deal of Spanish poetry in the last twenty-five years has been of truly appalling quality, but Lechner, (*El compromiso en la poesía española del siglo XX, part 2*) remarks that he has never read in the pages of *Ínsula* a single really negative poetry review, and this can be argued of poetry criticism in general. No wonder that Spanish writers either show their work to one another or write without hope of real feed-back.

The foregoing is not a complaint so much as an attempt to explain why debate about modernism and commitment in Spain should have been so extreme and have so influenced the development of the literature. The ingredients for an oscillation between elite and populist art were already in existence in Spain before the ideal of committed literature penetrated the country with the writings of Marxists, Fascists and others. It needed no Lukács to alert Spanish writers to the possible class basis of modernism. Spanish modernist literature was very much the product of a small literary elite whose politics were, broadly speaking, liberal, in the sense that the writers were neither aristocrats nor proletarians or peasants, but originated from the

67

(mostly provincial) urban middle class and were usually anti-clerical, reformist, pro-Republican, enlightened believers in parliamentary government, with little understanding of the economic theories of Socialism and with little or no overt hatred of capitalism or the concept of private property. This generalization is applicable to Unamuno, Miró, Pérez de Ayala, all the major poets (including Antonio Machado) and even to Baroja despite his dislike of parliamentary institutions. Liberal ideology has been proverbially weak in Spain, represented by a small insecure class always likely to be engulfed from the right or from the left by one extremism or another. The dispersal of the generation of modernist writers in 1936 expresses the fate of Spanish liberalism. The self-conscious elitism of Spanish modernist literature is an expression of an embattled isolation. Its parallel in the politics of the generation is the extremism of writers such as Unamuno and Ortega. Where European liberals advocate tolerance and pluralism, both Ortega and Unamuno tend to assert that individualism must be preserved even at the cost of freedom, or of ensuring that the masses continue in servitude.

It is not surprising that the champions of committed writing should have reacted so violently against such a literature. When the liberal tradition was destroyed on Franco's victory in 1939, a vacuum was left at the heart of Spanish life which could only be filled by one of two types of mutually reinforcing extremism: the official ideology, so obviously unconnected with social realities as to insult the intelligence even of its disseminators, and various kinds of left-wing extremism in discreet disguise. The Franco regime represented the triumph of hierarchical elitism, capitalism and nationalism, and its existence discredited every ideology but that which represented the alternative—Socialist collectivism. Under such circumstances, when nearly every reasonable and humane writer was likely to be a left-winger, modernist literature did not have a chance. So a rich and promising tradition was ignored for a committed anti-literature nostalgic for non-elitist modes of literary production, such as the oral poetic tradition or a conversational, anecdotal realism.

The sociology of Spanish literature is a fascinating and almost unexplored subject. An aspect I have not touched on here is the way in which proximity to western Europe means that modern Spanish writers are closely in touch with the latest fashions and experiments in French and other literatures. This proximity distorts Spanish literature in interesting ways. Writers in Spain have instant access to literary modes which do not really correspond to the level of development of Spanish society. Literary ideas and general ideology are thus constantly out of phase with the actual problems raised by everyday Spanish life. Romanticism arrives before rationalism and while Catholic absolutism is still more or less intact; the Paris–Madrid express brings *Das Kapital* while the mills and foundries are scarcely built; realism is barely established before it is engulfed by European modernism; anti-scientific irrationalism arrives ahead of the technology which generates it. This constant tension between ideology and social realities, between language and experience, explains the *bizarreness and originality of much modern Spanish literature. It also* explains why Spanish writers who are sensitive to new developments in European literature and thought, find themselves at odds with their own society. On the one hand there is literary culture, sophisticated, brilliant and somehow French, German or British. On the other hand there is 'reality', medieval, impoverished, half-African. This is how it has been seen by many Spanish writers. Little wonder that being an author generates an uneasy conscience or that the autonomy of literature is constantly challenged by those who try to close the gap that separates it from the realities of Spanish life.

Notes

Chapter One

(1) Many opposition works were, of course, printed outside Spain in order to avoid censorship; but their language, themes and structure are not radically different from opposition works printed in Spain. Unlike the USSR, the Franco censorship never applied to specific literary or artistic techniques or schools, and Spanish writers were never under official pressure to produce any particular type of literature. To this extent the censorship was artistically non-ideological.

(2) The term is discussed later in the chapter. Spanish is alone—to my knowledge—among the major European languages in having no word for literary modernism. Juan Ramón Jiménez's claim that the word *modernismo* really indicated a spirit of the age indicates dissatisfaction with the narrowness of the Spanish term.

(3) Written 1833 and reprinted in Max Aub, *La prosa española del siglo XIX: románticos* (Mexico, 1953), pp. 4–22.

(4) 'Towards an Understanding of Spanish Romanticism', MLR 58 (1963), pp. 190–5 (p. 193).

(5) 'Literatura' in *El Español*, 18th January, 1836, reprinted in *Artículos de crítica literaria*, edited by H. Grant and R. Johnson (Salamanca, 1964), pp. 73–7 (p. 77). For an account of the complex relationship between liberalism and Spanish romanticism, see V. Llorens Castillo, *Liberales y románticos* (Mexico, 1954), especially pp. 351–62. Romantic populism could be either radical or reactionary: exaltation of the *pueblo* or common people could be based either on nostalgia for the *ancien régime* or on the new democratic theories. This is also true of later versions of populism in Spain.

(6) Quoted in G. Díaz-Plaja, *Modernismo frente a noventayocho* (Madrid, 1951), p. 52.

(7) See *Obras completas*, 3 vols (Madrid, 1958–68), III, pp. 1439–54, especially 1452.

(8) See I. Zavala, *Ideología y política en la novela española del siglo XIX* (Salamanca, 1971), p. 198. The first example known to me of left-wing denunciations of aestheticism and subjectivism in literature as 'reac-

tionary' are to be found in Unamuno's socialist articles in the Bilbao *Lucha de Clases* in the period 1894–7. See his 'Sobre la regeneración del teatro español' (1896), reprinted in *Obras completas*, edited M. García Blanco, 16 vols (Madrid 1963–), III, 330–63, for an accessible account of his socialist arguments about literature. Like later left- and right-wing critics, Unamuno defended a *Volksgeist* theory of literature and claimed that works written by 'mere individuals' could never achieve the quality of 'collective' products like Lope's plays or medieval ballads.

(9) From the preface to *Gritos del combate* (Madrid, 1875).

(10) Quoted from the 12th edition of *Gritos del combate* (Madrid, 1914), pp. 314–15. Both Núñez de Arce and Campoamor were active conservatives.

(11) See however his famous distinction between 'magnificent, sonorous' poetry and 'natural, brief, laconic' poetry 'from the soul' in *Cartas literarias a una mujer* (1861).

(12) For a full discussion see the Pelican Guides to European literature series, *Modernism 1890–1930*, edited by M. Bradbury and J. McFarlane (London, 1976). It is symbolic of Hispanism's isolation that this exhaustive survey which encompasses Germany, Britain, the USA, France, Italy, Russia, Scandinavia and even Finland, has no reference in the main text to any Spanish writer except Lorca, Ortega and Echegaray (!) and only a biographical mention of Jiménez in the appendix. This is not surprising, since the existence of the Spanish term *modernismo*, roughly equivalent to 'symbolism', prevents the larger meaning of the word penetrating the language. It is interesting to note the circumlocutions used by Spanish writers to express the idea of modernism. Many, like Ortega and Machado, are aware of a continuity linking symbolism to surrealism, and it may be that Spanish critics' vague use of the word *vanguardia* arises from attempts to find a word for modernism. For the Portuguese use of the word, quite distinct from Spanish, see O. Maria Carpeaux's *As revoltas modernistas na literatura* (Rio de Janeiro, 1968).

(13) Hispanic terminology is under no obligation to imitate European counterparts—at least when there is a fundamental difference between Spanish and European phenomena. In this case the local terminology, to which some Hispanists attach much importance, does not define any clear literary quality. 'Generation' refers to the accident of more or less common birthdates; '98' refers to a non-literary event, the loss of Cuba in 1898. Literary terms should ideally refer to literary

qualities, not to the circumstances of the writer. A group of contemporaries from the same country will inevitably write about more or less the same problems, and it is possible to find an *a posteriori* justification for any literary label selected on historical grounds. The Spanish term 'Generation of 98' seems to me as useful as taking Gissing, Wells, Havelock Ellis, Hardy, James and Wilde and calling them, 'the Generation of 1899' on the grounds that all published important work in or around the year of the Boer War and none wrote like Symons or Dowson.

Chapter Two

(1) See *Arte y estado* by E. Giménez Caballero (Madrid, 1935). The military regime did produce fierce political reactions in literature from Unamuno (cf. *Cómo se hace una novela*) and Ramón del Valle-Inclán.

(2) First published Madrid, 1925. All my quotations are from the 6th *Revista de Occidente* edition (Madrid, 1960).

(3) José Díaz, *El nuevo romanticismo* (Madrid, 1930). José Díaz Fernández (1898–1941) campaigned vigorously against the Dictatorship of Primo, was editor of *Nueva Espana* and died in exile.

(4) *Veinte años de poesía española, 1939–1959* (Barcelona, 1960). For further remarks on Castellet's Marxist criticism see Chapter Four.

(5) *Poesia, realisme, història* (Barcelona, 1965), p. 89. This book echoes Machado in calling for a 'realist' poetry which would affirm 'an objective reality independent from ourselves'. (p. 69).

(6) All quotations from Machado are from the Losada edition of *Los complementarios* (Buenos Aires, 1957), except where stated.

(7) *Veinte años de poesía española*, p. 101.

(8) For Machado's more explicitly pro-Communist statements see *Prosas y poesías olvidadas de A. Machado*, edited by R. Marrast and R. Martínez-Lopez (Paris, 1964). Machado's eventual political position is perhaps best reflected in the following statement: 'El Partido Comunista español (os habla un hombre que no está afiliado a él y que dista mucho en teoría del puro marxismo) es una creación españolísima, un crisol de las virtudes populares.' ('The Spanish Communist Party [and these are the words of a man who is not affiliated to it and is a long way in theory from pure Marxism] is a highly Spanish creation, a crucible of popular virtues.') Machado's war-time speeches and poetry are patriotic and traditionalist in flavour, constantly referring to the popular uprising against the Napoleonic invasion. His war poems are collected in *Poesías de guerra*, edited by A. de Albornoz

(Puerto Rico, 1961). For some remarks on the traditionalism of Spanish Republican poetry see Chapter Three.

(9) *Los complementarios*, p. 114. The quotation is from Machado's speech to the Spanish Academy, written in 1931 but unpublished until 1951.

(10) Quoted in *Poesía*, 12th Austral edition, (Madrid, 1969), p. 262.

(11) 'Sobre una lírica comunista que pudiera venir de Rusia', *Octubre*, 1934, reprinted in *Los complementarios*, pp. 146–8.

(12) Such 'objectivism' is also a feature of Jorge Guillén's poetry, although the latter does not link it to a materialist conception of the world as is the case with other critics (and perhaps Machado as well). Jorge Guillén later wrote anti-Franco poetry from a vaguely liberal and elitist standpoint, cf. 'Potencia de Pérez' in his collection *Clamor* (1949–).

(13) *Arte y estado* (Madrid, 1935). For a full account of Giménez Caballero's ideas, and of *Falangista* literature in general, see J-C Mainer, *Falange y literatura* (Barcelona, 1971). Anti-modernist prejudice among Fascists was certainly less strong than among left-wingers. Febrile Fascist exaltations of the warrior life and of the state produce a much more convoluted kind of poetic rhetoric than did later Marxist realism.

(14) Valladolid, 1939. Despite the realist bias of Pemán's preface, the poem makes notable concessions to imagination. One section shows the infant Franco's cradle attended by guardian angels bearing a sword, a scales of Justice and 'a smile of goodness'. The poem is about a Christian crusade against the 'Jewish Communist Beast'. Nevertheless Pemán declared himself a lifelong liberal in an interview given to *Triunfo*, 20th December, 1972.

(15) 'Una generación poética (1920–36)', written 1948 and reprinted in *Obras completas*, (Madrid, 1972–), vol IV, pp. 653–76 (footnote to page 655).

(16) Quoted in J. Lechner, *El compromiso en la poesía española del siglo XX*, part one (Leiden, 1968), p. 159.

Chapter Three

(1) Perhaps Cernuda may be said also to have rejected modernism, although not for political reasons. Cernuda's Communism, which was short lived, had no impact on his poetry, but after *Donde habite el olvido* (1934) his poetry almost totally abandons the complex language

of his earlier works, to the extent that it often turns into a kind of dignified but stilted prose.

(2) For a collection of left-wing War ballads see *Romancero general de la guerra civil* (Valencia, 1937).

(3) Prologue to *El poeta en la calle* (Paris, 1966), an anthology of Alberti's 'civic' (i.e. political) poetry between 1931 and 1965.

(4) From 'La familia' (1934), idem, p. 36.

(5) 'Poética de Juan Panadero', in *Coplas de Juan Panadero* (1949–53), idem, p. 200.

(6) '18 de julio 1937' (first anniversary of the 'People's War' against Franco), from the series *Capital de la gloria*, reprinted in *Poesías completas* (Buenos Aires, 1961), p. 414.

(7) *Obras completas*, (Buenos Aires, 1960), p. 210.

(8) For an anthology of 'social poetry' see *Antología de la poesía social*, edited by Leopoldo Luis (Madrid, 1965). It contains a number of declarations by poets about the need for 'rehumanized' poetry—i.e. political poetry—and for an end to 'aestheticism' etc. A full account of the publications of the *poesía social* movement is to be found in J. Lechner, *El compromiso en la poesía española del siglo XX*, part two, *1939 a 1974* (Leiden, 1975), pp. 66–85. To judge by the author's statistics, the highpoint of the movement was 1954–65, after which date there was a dramatic decline in the output of politicized verse. Few people were distracted by the euphemistic title of the 'social poetry' movement: 'This social poetry has not been social but political. Poetry in opposition to the government' (L. Jiménez Martos, in 'Literatura social: ¿podemos definirla?', in Supplement number 19 of *Cuadernos para el Diálogo*, edited by E. García Rico, (Madrid, 1971), p. 7. Gabriel Celaya thought that political poetry of the left was a reaction to a right-wing provocation. In his view, the first wave of committed poetry had come from writers like Pemán, and from magazines like Garcilaso. (*Cuadernos*, ibid, p. 24).

(9) 'Interior', *Poesías completas* (Madrid, 1968), pp. 53–4. All quotations from Celaya are from this edition. Celaya was at this time an active member of the then clandestine Communist Party.

(10) *Hacia la inmensa mayoría* (Buenos Aires, 1962), p. 122. All quotations from Otero's work are from this left-wing anthology.

(11) From 'Poética' in *Nueve novísimos*, edited by J. M. Castellet (Barcelona, 1970), p. 59. Castellet's chastened prologue acknowledges the fact that the 'theoretical bases of realism began to become a nightmare' around 1962. The anthology contains poems by

M. Vázquez Montalbán, A. Martñez Sarrión, J-M Alvárez, Félix de Azúa, Pedro Gimferrer, Vicente Molina-Moix, Guillermo Carnero, Ana Maria Moix and Leopoldo Panero. The '*poéticas*' preceding each selection generally contain defences of aestheticism or rejections of the idea of social responsibility.

Chapter Four

(1) See *Cazador en el alba y otras imaginaciones* (Barcelona, 1971), a selection of Ayala's avant-garde stories from the pre-War period. Such writing explains the fierceness of the realist reaction: Ayala wrote in 1929 that the artist assembles his work from ideas and sensations which form the 'components of his work, and are completely useless and correspond to nothing in the natural order of the world', ibid, p. 23.

(2) 'Figurines literarios' (1899), reprinted in *Escritos de juventud*, edited M. Longares (Madrid, 1972), pp. 230–4.

(3) See F. Baeza, *Baroja y su mundo* (Madrid, 1961), pp. 59–60, for an account by Baroja's nephew. The author points out (p. 60) that the rabidly Fascist and anti-Semitic tract *Comunistas, Judíos, farsantes y demás ralea* (Valladolid, 1938), printed in Baroja's name, was in fact compiled and published without Baroja's knowledge, probably by Giménez Caballero, from remarks made by characters in several of his novels over a long period. Its publication may have encouraged Fascists to overlook Baroja's anti-clericalism on his return to Spain after the Civil War.

(4) *Obras escogidas de Valle-Inclán* (Madrid, 1967), p. 640.

(5) For a detailed account of the *novela social* movement, with summaries of the major novels, see P. Gil Casado, *La novela social española* (Madrid, 1968). On the movement, see also E. G. de Nora, *La novela española contemporánea 1898–1960* (Madrid, 1958); J. M. Castellet (editor), '*Coloquio Internacional sobre la novela en Formentor*' in *Cuadernos del Congreso por la Libertad de la Cultura*, number 38 (September–October, 1959); E. García Rico (editor), *Literatura y política: en torno al realismo español, Cuadernos para el Diálogo*, Supplement number 19, (Madrid, 1971).

(6) P. Gil Casado, *op. cit.*, p. viii.

(7) *La revolución y la crítica de la cultura* (Barcelona, 1970), p. 148. Cf. also García Hortelano's remark: 'our position is as "committed" as

reality allows', interview to *Claridades*, Supplement of 29th October, 1961.

(8) 'De la objetividad al objeto', *Papeles de Son Armadans*, V, XV, pp. 308–32.

(9) *El Jarama*, fifth edition (Barcelona, 1961), p. 364. First published 1956.

(10) J. García Hortelano, *Nuevas amistades*, fourth edition (Barcelona, 1965), p. 92. First published 1959.

(11) A. Ferres, *La piqueta* (Barcelona, 1959), p. 96.

(12) For an excellent account of the shortcomings and collapse of Spanish socialist realism, see Juan Goytisolo, 'Literatura y eutanasia', in *El furgón de cola* (Paris, 1967), pp. 45–58. One of Goytisolo's complaints is that the social novel failed to utilize irony and humour—the long-standing Spanish satirical tradition was never exploited by the authors of social novels. The solemnity of social literature is only an aspect of the uniformity of tone and absence of complex perspectives within social novels and poems. But humour itself was under suspicion in Spain as a type of escapism. In a study of 'right-wing' theatre, J. Monleón claims that 'the "theatre of humour" has been the refuge of the best right-wing theatre since the Civil War', *30 años de teatro de la derecha* (Barcelona, 1971). This stigma seems to have attached itself to all humorous writing in the period.